Build Your Own
Information Literate School

Carol Koechlin
Sandi Zwaan

Hi Willow Research & Publishing
2004

Hi Willow Research and Publishing
312 South 1000 East
Salt Lake City UT 84102

Distributed by:
LMC Source
P.O. Box 131266
Spring TX 77393
800-873-3043
sales@lmcsource.com

ISBN: 0-931510-89-9

Contents

List of Figures

Introduction

Why Build Your Own: Information Literate School?

Leaders in the world of education have suggested for some time now that those in the business of teaching should develop strategies to ensure that students will be well equipped to deal with their world in the future. This is not a new concept. We know that students need to have the skills to "do life" as well as "do school." What is notable is that we expect it will be a much more complex world that our students will face in the future.

How do we prepare students for life in the 21st century? We know that information is acknowledged as a resource and people with high-level information skills are very marketable. Two attributes for success in the future that seem to repeatedly float to the top are critical thinking and information processing. As a result of an international study (Cogan and Derriccott, 1998), a set of principles for educational policy for the 21st century was developed. The first two of these principles were very highly recommended:

- Support the teaching of subject matter in a manner that encourages children to think critically.

- Emphasize students' ability to critically assess information in an increasingly media-based society. [1]

In 1998 the American Association of School Libraries developed *Information Power*. This document provides a set of nine information literacy standards and principles for addressing the needs of schools in the 21st century, as well as providing a vision for implementation. "The school library media specialist can use the information literacy standards for student learning to create and maintain a program for a broad learning community - students, teachers, administrators, parents, and the neighbourhood - that will support lifelong learning."[2]

The Canadian School Library Association has just published standards for information literacy. This document similarly envisions an extended learning environment to address future needs." *Members of a learning community constantly gain new knowledge and develop new skills. In their role of preparing children for society, schools are responsible for teaching children how to adapt to change and how to make decisions and solve problems based on accurate and authentic information. Critical thinking skills are essential to evaluate information creatively and responsibly to solve problems."* [3]

In spite of these recommendations, standards, and vision statements, emphasis today is on student achievement in the traditional three R's. Teacher accountability and the ranking of

---

[1] John J. Cogan and Ray Derricott. *Citizenship for the 21st Century: An International Perspective on Education.* London: Kogan Page, 1998.
Multidimensional Citizenship: Educational Policy for the Twenty-first Century
http://hkied.education.umn.edu/hkied-um/citizen.html#summary
[2] AASL. *Information Literacy Standards for Student Learning.* Chicago: AASL, 1998.
[3] CSLA and ATLC. *Achieving Information Literacy: Standards for School Library Programs in Canada.* Ottawa: CSLA and CSLA, 2003.

schools is front page rather than achievement in the information skills that futurists and employers state are necessary for students in the 21st century. Perhaps with a little creativity we can link all these priorities.

Is it possible to teach students to be critical thinkers and effective users of information and information technologies and at the same time improve their overall achievement levels?

Can educators prepare their students for the future with the information skills that will be so vital to their success, and still address the needs of current curriculum structures? e.g. standards-based curriculum, criterion assessment, constructivism, co-operative learning, cross-curricular programs and integration of the arts, and information technology etc.?

A body of important research has quietly but persistently grown which demonstrates the link between strong school library programs and student achievement. Evidence has been gathered in over 4,000 schools across United States and, time after time, the research results are consistent. In their book *Powering Achievement*, Keith Curry Lance and David Loertscher suggest a simple formula for school communities engaged in school-wide improvement to enhance student achievement:

> *First, create a quality information-rich and technology rich environment easily accessible by students and teachers.*

> *Second, employ professional and support personnel who provide leadership and tireless partnering.*

Lance and Loertscher suggest that when schools invest in their school library to create such an environment, the research shows that they can also expect:

- *Capable and avid readers*

- *Learners who are information literate*

- *Teachers who are partnering with the library media professional to create high quality learning experiences*

> *When these things happen, scores can be expected to be 10% - 20% higher than in schools without this investment.[4]*

Herein lie important foundations for the building of an information literate school. Students need critical thinking and information skills for immediate improvement and for their success in the future. We need to invest in the school library media center staffing, program, collections and facilities. To maximize results, we must to develop a collaborative culture in the school so teachers and library media specialists have opportunities to work together as partners to design excellent learning experiences that necessitate learners to think critically as they work with information. To facilitate this process, schools require a school library media center with a fulltime, well-qualified library media specialist who will lead the building process. The results

---

[4] David Loertscher and Keith Lance. *Powering Achievement* * 2nd Edition: *School Libraries Make a Difference.* San Jose, CA.: Hi Willow Research and Publishing, 2003. Available at www.lmcsource.com

will be information literate teachers, students, and school communities prepared for learning, working and playing in the 21st century.

What are the criteria for creating such a learning environment?

© a school-wide information skills continuum.

© a consistent research model.

© equitable access to information and information skills programs.

© collaborative partnerships between teachers and library media specialists.

© a networked school library that provides the information infrastructure for the school.

© optimization of the potential of information-based technologies as tools to enhance performance for students, staff, and administration.

© investment in high quality, needs, and interest-based school library collections.

© relevant and authentic learning tasks that require analysis and synthesis and provide opportunities for transfer of skills and knowledge.

©   staff and students who practice academic honesty and value information.

© students, teachers, and a school community, who understand the meaning and importance of information literacy and strive to achieve it.

© administration and lead teachers who engage the staff in a cycle of inquiry to improve teaching and learning.

About this book

In preparation for writing this book, we collected and examined standards and expectations in all disciplines from across Canada and the United States. We identified standards and expectations that require information skills. What we discovered was an abundance of standards requiring knowledge and expertise with information skills. This pattern is consistent across the continent. As we sought out examples that overtly represented these skills, and their different levels of sophistication, we discovered that many of the expectations and standards require very high levels of evaluation, analysis and synthesis of information.

We then examined a broad sampling of the information literacy standards and expectations used in schools across North America. We clustered them into stages of the research/inquiry process and then compared them to the types of information skills required in the content areas of the curriculum. Our next task was to identify the commonalities and exceptions and ensure that the continuum presented in *Build Your Own Information Literate School* includes all those necessitated by the content standards.

For the sake of organization, we have used the research model that we developed through our own practice in school library programs. We hope that users of this book will not feel restricted to this research framework. We invite you to look beyond the model and concentrate on development of information skills as they can be applied to your own research or information processing structure.

We have created sample tasks for the basic skills needed at each stage of the research process. We have attempted to demonstrate growth of the mastery of each skill by breaking down each information skill.

Each skill has been considered at three levels of sophistication. Note that the complexity of the skill development is not necessarily tied to grade level. Rather, the intent is for the practitioner to decide which level the students are ready for by considering past experience with the skill, readiness, and age appropriateness of the technique being modelled. You will notice that while the skill level may be **Novice** often the level of the activity is junior or intermediate. Conversely, the **Apprentice** or **InfoStar** level examples could be primary or junior (See next page). Note that all skills are taught in the context of a curriculum topic and are critical to the success of students in meeting content standards.

We wish to emphasize that the use of information technology is not considered a separate skill but rather a tool to enhance access, management and communication of information. Information technologies are integrated into each of the tasks, where appropriate, rather than separated into specific lessons. It is our intention to model that the use of information technologies can enhance the learning, make information processing more efficient, and the learning more effective. There is no doubt that to prepare our students for their 21st century world we need to ensure that they are computer savvy. The trick, of course, is to design rich learning experiences for students and provide them with opportunities to discover what is the best tool for each information task.

Questions and questioning may be the most powerful technologies of all.
Jamie McKenzie. *Beyond Technology: Questioning, Research and the Information Literate School,* FNO Press: Bellingham, Washington, 2000.

InfoSkill Levels

Novice Learner

This is a first experience with the skill. The approach is usually to model the application of the skill while verbalising the process. We want the students to be familiar with the thought processes they will use when applying this skill. We have often used some form of simple collaborative activity to reinforce the learning and allow students to safely demonstrate their understanding of the skill and the content. Students will need opportunity to practice this Novice level of skill before they are ready to go on to try something more complex.

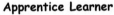

Apprentice Learner

Students understand and can demonstrate success at the Novice level. Now they are ready for applications where the skill increases in complexity or scope and/or requires some independence. The nature of the task and the sophistication of the content will drive the complexity of the skill application. The skill is still modeled through a lesson carefully structured to build self-reliance. The apprentice learner then demonstrates ability to apply the skill in a specific context and use reflective tools to help develop metacognition. The Apprentices need many opportunities to practice before they own the skill.

InfoStar

Students have demonstrated understanding of the basic skill set at this level and are asked to apply it independently and creatively. Another level of complexity may be introduced or students may be asked to develop a plan, carry out a task using the skill, and then evaluate their success. Again, the nature of the task and the sophistication of the content will drive the complexity of the skill application. At this level students will demonstrate their command of the skill and their ability to transfer learning from one situation or subject area to another. InfoStars are information literate lifelong learners.

In this book we provide a continuum of information skills and processes to help you build an information literate school. We believe that the model lessons provided will help equip students with the skills they need for success, not only now while in school, but also in the future. The intent of this publication is to provide educators with a handy reference tool, not a step-by-step recipe book for teaching information skills. Use it as you would an encyclopaedia. Plan to teach information skills at the critical moment when they are needed most.

Just in Time

Information skills are often embedded in the content standards that our classroom teachers use to frame their units of study. We must analyze each curriculum expectation to determine which information skills will be required to achieve it. It isn't always obvious. Information skills are often assumed or lost in the focus on content. Look for trigger words or phrases such as evaluate, recognize the importance of, debate, assume a point of view, investigate, communicate, make a judgment, state a conclusion, interpret, explore, compare, discover a relationship, identify a trend. These words alert us to the embedded information skills students need to be successful with the task.

Some expectations begin with a low level instruction such as "identify," and at first glance appear simple, but then go on to require much higher and more complicated levels of processing. Others overtly require high-level analysis and critical thinking, but students need to complete several other layers of processing before attempting them.

Deconstructing Content Standards

Students will investigate daily life in ancient civilizations.
This sounds simple, but actually requires the knowledge and application of a number of information skills. Students must locate appropriate resources. Next they need to find the information specific to daily life. In order to be able to do this they need to know how to use the index, table of contents, and glossary. They must be skilled at reading, viewing and listening to non-fiction text. They must be able to use titles, subtitles, captions and sidebars. They need to be able to read and interpret a variety of visuals, pictures, illustrations, charts, graphs and so on.

Students will compare and contrast the product information contained in advertisements with instruction manuals and warrantees.
This is a more complex standard requiring a number of skills and steps. The students must first gather and evaluate the sources for each of the items being compared. They next identify the data relevant to their need, then determine which aspects they will compare, and establish criteria for comparison. Having done this, they will sort their information for each item by aspect. Next they identify the similarities and differences so that they are able to ready to apply the criteria to make comparison and contrast statements.

Students determine impact of technological development on humans and the environment.
This requires a very high level of critical thinking. First they need to consider the causes and effects of the situation over a period of time. Second, they must take into account all the relevant perspectives of those affected, analyzing the positive and negative spin-offs based on their predetermined criteria. Next, they must weigh these findings and make links to other related knowledge or experiences they have had. Having done this, they will be ready to determine and evaluate the impact.

Focus on the information skills needed for the expectation. After the initial teaching of each skill, provide students with many opportunities to practice them. Consciously and strategically create or take advantage of situations to review, revisit, and re-enforce information skills in logical sequence and in the context of relevant curriculum. Keep track of class, division, and school progress. Introduce or review skills "just in time" for a relevant curriculum application, not "just in case" they might use it some day.

How do you make this work for you?

Build a repertoire of strategies so you can apply them strategically, for skill development, as they are needed. Dissect the standard or task to determine the information skills required to enable understanding and building of content knowledge. When a standard or task calls for students to make comparisons, for example, reach into your repertoire bank to find just the right strategy to match student experience and best enable content learning. Work with the classroom teacher to determine which information skills the students will need to review, practice, or to be taught, in order to experience success with the task at hand. Look closely at the task definition and peel back the layers to discover the steps required to enable students to achieve it. Sequence and spiral the learning experiences so students are able to apply the targeted skill when they need it. (See the box on p. x)

How else can I use this book?

©   a framework for school-wide information skills.

©   a formula for improvement of student achievement.

©   a tool to help determine the requisite skills for a given standard.

©   a resource for ideas and strategies for classroom teachers and library media specialists.

©   a source of student organizers, checklists, and rubrics.

©   a catalyst for school wide collaboration.

©   a model for effective integration of information and communication technologies.

©   a source for ideas for actions on which to document evidence-based practice.

©   the starting point for action research in the library media center.

Documenting Success in the Information Literate School

Assessment is an integral component of all teaching and learning. In an information literate school, the library media specialists must be involved, or better still lead, the assessment portfolio for their area of expertise. Assessment is often narrowly interpreted as only measurement of student performance, and while that is one goal, to be sure, there is so much more to assessment. We can use assessment strategies to measure student achievement of the minute and also to determine progress over the long term. Assessment informs teachers, students, parents, and administrators of the progress of the individual student as well as the student body as a whole. Assessment information can be used by all stakeholders to set goals for improvement.

Once informed as to how well their performance stacks up against desired standards, the students can develop personal plans for improvement. Parents can plan how to help their children meet the targeted goals.

Teachers can also use this information to assess how well teaching and assessment strategies worked. If we hope to be the best possible facilitators of learning, our teaching should be a constant cycle of design, reflect, rethink, and redesign. The questions included in the *Reflect, Rethink, Redesign* section of each task will help prompt our thoughts as we go through the process of assessing our teaching and learning strategies and gathering evidence of our successes.

Administrators can use assessment records to provide information to help make decisions around staffing, school initiatives, budget, and school improvement. With all these demands on the assessment process, it stands to reason that schools need to gather as many different kinds of assessment data as possible before drawing conclusions and making changes. Dr. David Loertscher argues that there are three major types of evidence to be collected in a school in order to provide a more holistic view of the library media program. Applying the strength of the triangle we have adopted Loertscher's theory of *Triangulation of Data-Driven Practice.* [5] We suggest considering effectiveness of teaching and learning experiences in the school library and the classroom from three perspectives.

Learner Level

We have developed criteria, in Gathering Evidence of Understanding, for measuring student success. These criteria can be used for developing tools such as rubrics, checklists, and rating scales.

Teaching Unit Level

The criteria we described in this category provide guidelines for assessing the success of the teaching and learning experience. Gather evidence both informally, from conversations and observations, and formally, using collaboration logs, case studies, and reflective journals.

Organization Level

At this level we have included criteria for assessing the effectiveness of the learning environment. They encompass the physical space, resources, equipment and ambience.

[5] David V. Loertscher and Ross Todd. *We Boost Achievement!: Evidence-Based Practice for School Library Media Specialists*. Salt Lake City UT: Hi Willow Research & Publishing, 2003 (dist. by LMC Source at www.lmcsource.com).

Each task models documenting evidence from one or more of these perspectives. Collecting this kind of data at the school level can be powerful. This is tangible evidence you can use to negotiate time, budget, and staffing. In doing so, make links to the current research. (Lance, Loertscher 2003[6] and Haycock 2003[7]) This research shows how much school libraries and library programs contribute to student achievement. Share this, along with your grassroots evidence at faculty meetings, in school newsletters, in annual reports, with parents and colleagues. Celebrate your success and capitalise on its effects. Work together with your school community to build your own information literate school.

> *"Although many people demand statistical data to support research findings, it is important not to forget that people also respond strongly to data in narrative form – stories, case studies or brief scenarios."*
> Dianne Oberg, *Looking for the evidence: Do school libraries improve student achievement?*
> School Libraries in Canada, Volume 22 Number 2, 2002.

> *"Restructuring schools for the information age has not reached its full potential in any country. It is time to put the expertise of teacher-librarians to work on the critical task of redesigning schools. Teacher-librarians play a vital role in creating inquiry learning that prepares students for work, citizenship and daily living in the information age."*
> Carol Kuhlthau, IASL Conference, Auckland, New Zealand, 2001.

> *The principal must have the district's support, just as the librarian must have the principal's. The elements of success here are nested inside one another like those Russian decorative eggs.*
> Gary Hartzell, The White House Conference on School Libraries, Washington D.C., 2002.

> *Strong school library media programs make a difference in academic achievement. That is if you were setting out a balanced meal for a learner, the school library media program would be part of the main course, not the butter on the bread.*
> Keith Curry Lance and David Loertscher, *Powering Achievement: School Library Media Programs Make a Difference*, 2002.

> *The school library provides information and ideas that are fundamental to functioning in today's information and knowledge based society. The school library equips students with life-long learning skills and develops the imagination, enabling them to live as responsible citizens.*
> UNESCO/IFLA School Library Manifesto, 2000.

---

[6] David V. Loertscher and Keith Lance. *Powering Achievement: School Library Media Programs Make a Difference: The Evidence.* 2nd Edition. San Jose, Cal.: Hi Willow, 2002.
[7] Ken Haycock. *The Crisis in Canada's School Libraries: The Case for Reform and Reinvestment.* http://www.publishers.ca/pages/HaycockACP2_v2.pdf

David Loertscher's Introduction

This book is simply the best book on teaching information literacy to date.

When the authors' book *InfoTasks* was published by Pembroke in 2001, I could see that these authors had extensive experience in teaching information literacy in ways not usually done in the United States, but their approach would be enormously helpful. Thus, after several intense planning sessions, the content and layout of this book was developed.

It **is not** a book to teach the skills sequentially!
It **is** a book for all grade levels and even for adults.
It should be considered more like an encyclopedia.

Do three things after briefly reading through this book to get its design and layout scheme:
1. Determine the skill learners need at a given moment in time as they try to reach a state standard.
2. Determine whether the learners are novices, apprentices, or InfoStars in their level of sophistication regardless of their grade level.
3. Find the information literacy task in this book and you will find a gold mine of recommendations for teaching across the curriculum.

Another feature of this book is its recommended assessment techniques for every information skill taught whether in social studies, language arts, or other content areas. These recommendations are at three levels: the learner level, the teaching unit level, and the organization level. It is not enough any more to just say that: "We taught 25 information literacy lessons last week."

Thus, this book is far beyond the information literacy skill model teaching that has been so popular in the U.S. And it also covers in a wonderful way, information literacy skills that have often been ignored such as analysis and synthesis.

Enjoy.

Part 1: Define and Clarify

The seed of inquiry is planted and the wonderment begins. Although students are engaged and excited about their new learning adventure they can also experience a great deal of discomfort at this early stage of the process. One way to counteract this possible unrest is to help students understand that this is a natural part of the research process.

Right from the beginning students need to understand the purpose and value of the different stages of the research process. The exploration of background information and the search for a personal research topic can feel chaotic and messy. They must have lots of experiences with the topic so that they are able to brainstorm, formulate questions, develop a focus and begin locating useful data. The tasks in this section will help prepare your students with the skills required to define and clarify their research quest.

(p2) Understand the Research Process
   Novice: Learning Map
   Apprentice: Attributes of Stages
   InfoStar: Personal Model

(p4) Explore a Topic
   Novice: Explore through Senses
   Apprentice: Explore through a Variety of Selected Resources
   InfoStar: Explore through Databases

(p8) Define a Research Topic
   Novice: Narrow to Categories
   Apprentice: Narrow to Categories and Sub Categories
   InfoStar: Narrowing Using Technology

(p12) Develop Questions
   Novice: Model Questioning
   Apprentice: Generate Questions Using a Question Matrix
   InfoStar: Generate Questions by Purpose

(p14) Keywords
   Novice: Identify Search Features
   Apprentice: Expand Keywords and Phrases
   InfoStar: Develop a Search Plan

(p16) Develop a Plan
   Novice: Model the Process
   Apprentice: Follow a Research Plan Independently
   InfoStar: Create a Research Plan

InfoSkill:
Understand the Research Process
Students will understand that research is a process of inquiry. They will discover the importance of the research process for personal and workplace applications.

Skill Discussion

The research process is an instructional strategy. As with other learning strategies it is important to help students understand the relevance of what they are doing. It is therefore very important to spend some time building connections between the research process and familiar student experiences. It is vital that students learn to not only execute but also value each stage of the research process. They also need to realize how stages of the process are interdependent; that too little or inaccurate data will impede analysis, that inadequate analysis of information will have a negative impact on their attempts to synthesize...

Students depend on the skills they learn in their research experiences to be able to process information in all disciplines. The skills of the research process are life-long learning skills. Students need to master these skills and transfer and apply them independently across the curriculum and in their personal lives.

For ultimate transfer of skills from one discipline to another in the early years, a consistent research model is requisite.

Link Up

- American Association of School Librarians, Guidelines and Standards http://www.ala.org/aasl/ip_implementation.html

- Noodle Tools, The Building Blocks of Research http://www.noodletools.com/debbie/literacies/information/1over/infolit1.html

- Access OLA, Information Studies K-12, Ontario School library Association http://www.accessola.org/action/positions/info_studies/html/research.html

- School District 23 Central Okanogan, The Research Quest: A Student Guide http://sd23.bc.ca/students/researchquestnew.html

Novice: *Learning Map*

Teach through Language Arts

Group students and provide them with a large piece of chart paper and markers. Instruct groups to discuss the occupation "researcher" and make a large sketch of what they think a researcher looks like. Post the charts and look for common attributes. List these attributes on a chart. Likely you will discover they say things like white coat, glasses, clipboard etc. Discuss findings. Pose the question "What do researchers really have in common?" Inform students that this question is their information problem and they will need to develop a plan for solving it. Brainstorm for actions students feel they will need to take and align their ideas, in their words, with the research model that you plan to implement. e.g.

> © Define and clarify
> © Locate and Retrieve
> © Select Process and Record
> © Analyze
> © Synthesize
> © Share and Use
> © Reflect Transfer and Apply
> Koechlin, Zwaan

Inform students that this chart is like a learning "road map". Model and discuss each stage of the research process as the students embark on this inquiry. Develop focus questions and decide on places and people that can help them discover information about researchers. Set up strategies for processing the data they gather, then share and discuss their findings about real world researchers.

Gathering Evidence of Understanding

Have students make a flow chart of the research process they just implemented. Ask students to explain what they did at each step and why. Students should be able to chart and label stages of the research process. They should be able to explain how the process helps keep them on track and informs them of what to do next just as a road map does.

Novice Adaptation

Have students draw pictures of themselves engaged in a step of the research process. The pictures can be mounted on the cover of their research folder.

Take digital photographs of them working throughout the process and display them on a bulletin board with the steps of the research process to help students understand that they are using the same skills professional researchers use in the real world.

Apprentice: *Attributes of Stages*

Teach through Science and Language Arts

Introduce students to analogies. Use familiar examples. Read Eric Carle's, *The Very Hungry Caterpillar*. Discuss and chart the stages of metamorphosis. Review the stages of the research process. Develop an analogy between the development of a butterfly and the stages of the research process. Help students to come up with similarities for each stage.

Form small groups and provide each group of students with an analogy to develop.
How is the research process like a ladder? a menu?, a river?, a set of keys?, a cheese?, a cake?, a spring?, and a diary? Share ideas and post them.

Gathering Evidence of Understanding

Instruct students to create a visual flow chart of the research process incorporating analogies.

InfoStar: *Personal Model*

Teach through Careers

Review the research process by asking small groups of students to create a diagram that shows the steps of a process needed to make a personal decision. Each group has a different task e.g. purchasing a printer, renting an apartment, investing savings, planning a holiday etc. Share diagrams, look for common elements, and make links to the research process.

Gathering Evidence of Understanding

Instruct students to individually create a visual representation of the process they use when conducting research. Look for evidence of all major steps in the process as well as understanding of the cyclical/recursive nature of research. Critical components are questioning, reflection, evaluation, analysis, making personal meaning and goal setting.

InfoStar Adaptation

Present the question, "How will research skills help in the workplace?" Provide students with copies of employability skills. Instruct students to examine these skills and highlight those that are routinely applied in the research process. Have students look in the career section of a newspaper for a job advertisement that seems to require information-processing skills. Instruct students to write a letter of application for the position that highlights the pertinent research skills they have that would be valuable to the employer. Remind students to apply their knowledge of the research process and the links to employability skills employers are looking for:
•Scans 2000 the Workforce Skills Web Site http://www.scans.jhu.edu/NS/HTML/Index.htm
•Employability Skills 2000 http://www2.conference board.ca/education/learning-tools/employability-skills.htm

Notes:
Reflect, Rethink, Redesign

© Do students understand that a research model is a learning map?

© Are students able to analogize the process?

© How can I make the process more concrete for students?

© Do students understand they will be assessed at every stage in the research process?

© Are they aware that they may have to loop back to a previous stage at some points? e.g. When the quantity of information is inadequate they will have to go back to the locate and retrieve stage.

Documenting the Evidence

Teaching Unit Level

© Evidence of student independence with the process.

© Less teaching time spent on access and management skills.

© More time to spend on helping students process information.

© Students and co-teachers value all stages of research.

© Students include all stages in the process.

© Research process is applied to other information problems.

InfoSkill:

Explore a Topic

Students will use a variety of strategies to explore a topic in preparation for research.

Skill Discussion

This first step in research is crucial to research success. Students are often discouraged by research projects because they find the topic too broad, too narrow or of no personal interest to them. At the beginning introduce the topic by engaging students and firing up their passion and curiosity.

Students must have a good working knowledge of the topic before they can create questions or select effective keywords. They must have been immersed in the general topic to become familiar with the language of the topic. The time spent up front providing exploration activities will pay huge dividends later in the research cycle.

Exploring with Your Senses, Fig. 1

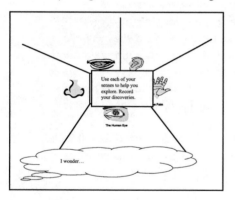

Link Up

Selected Web Directories:

- Librarians' Index to the Internet: www.lii.org
- World Wide Web Virtual Library: http://vlib.org
- Academic Info: www.academicinfo.co
- Yahoo Educational Directories
  http://dir.yahoo.com/Education/Web_Directories/

Novice: *Explore through Senses*

Teach through Science

Students are preparing to study plants that provide food. Select a seasonal plant such as the pumpkin and bring some to class. Instruct students to use all their senses to discover fascinating information about pumpkins. Provide a variety of activities to help students learn how to observe and record their discoveries. Keep a large class chart of student observations.

- *Read with your eyes.* e.g. plant, stem, root, leaves, fruit, colors, size, shape
- *Read with your hands.* e.g. textures, temperature, shape, size, weight
- *What do our ears help us to discover about pumpkins?* e.g. songs, video, listening to stories
- *How does our nose help us to know about pumpkins?* Smell of pumpkin flesh, pies, seeds cooking...
- *What can we tell by tasting?* e.g. fried or baked seeds, pies, cookies, muffins, soup, sweet, spicy, smooth, crunchy...(Be cautious of allergies and hygiene.)

Provide students with an organizer so they can also keep track of their new knowledge about pumpkins. Help students to find accurate terminology or to create effective illustrations to record their discoveries.

Gathering Evidence of Understanding

In a debriefing conference with students ask them to explain how their senses helped them to make discoveries about pumpkins. They should be able to articulate how each of their senses helped them discover something new about pumpkins. Now ask students if they have some curiosity or unanswered questions about pumpkins. Chart the student questions and set up activities to help them discover the answers using both print and electronic resources.

Novice Adaptation

Prepare a letter and senses organizer, such as *Exploring with Your Senses, Fig. 1,* for students to take home. Instruct the caregiver to find an item/artifact the student is unfamiliar with and follow the organizer to help the child practice the new skills of using senses to explore a topic.

Apprentice: Explore Through a Variety of Selected Resources

Teach through Social Studies

Prepare an overarching question to focus the big ideas of the unit e.g. *What are the relationships between immigrants today and early North American settlers?* Make a generous investment in exploratory activities. This is a messy stage of thinking for students. They need many opportunities to use their observation and questioning skills. This stage gives the students base-line knowledge and background to link their new learning to.

Students need stimulation to help them make connections between overall key ideas and their own experiences. What you want to do is set up a pinball effect then help students to sort these new ideas and make connections. Give them experiences with:

• Selected picture books and novels
• The arts - music, dance, theatre etc.
• Video clips and news broadcasts
• Guests and interviews
• Excursions both real and virtual (video)
• Food and customs
• Skimming books, magazines, newspapers
• Primary sources
• Browsing selected websites

Gathering Evidence of Understanding

Instruct students to create a pinball type web recording the key ideas and connections they have discovered through exploratory activities. Students should be able to chart major elements of life for early settlers and today's immigrants by using arrows and colors to begin making connections and discovering relationships. Have students identify, by highlighting, the ideas they are most interested in exploring further.

Apprentice Adaptations

Have students create a trivia game with the data and relationships they have discovered.

InfoStar: Explore through Databases

Teach through World Studies

To prepare students for an investigation of the effectiveness of international treaties for the protection of human rights, provide them with exploratory activities using online Web directories (webographies). Students will need an organizer so they can keep track of their journey and easily return to websites once they have decided on a focus for their investigation. The Web directory list will help students to connect to relevant issues and provide them with reliable links. Encourage students to keep jotting down thoughts and key ideas as they skim hits and browse articles.

Documenting the Evidence

Instruct students to revisit all their jotted notes from the exploration of directories. Have students use highlighters and different colored pens to continue to reflect on the topic and identify connections as they make them. Students should now be ready to develop questions to guide their inquiry. If they are still not keen on what they have discovered they should return to the directories and explore some different paths.

Notes:
Reflect, Rethink, Redesign

© Have I provided effective activities to focus exploratory experiences? e.g. a list of new vocabulary to look/listen for and define.
© Do students have a working knowledge of the new vocabulary?
© Were students exposed to a variety of media so that all learning styles were included?

Documenting the Evidence

Teaching Unit Level
Students:
© Are engaged with the topic.
© Know the basic 5Ws for this topic.
© Can create a visual representation of the topic.
© Can make a clear transition into next stage of the project.

Organization Level
© There are adequate and appropriate materials to support ESL learners;
© A variety of good resources on the topic; and
© Sufficient computer workstations.

Notes:

Exploring with Your Senses (Fig.1)

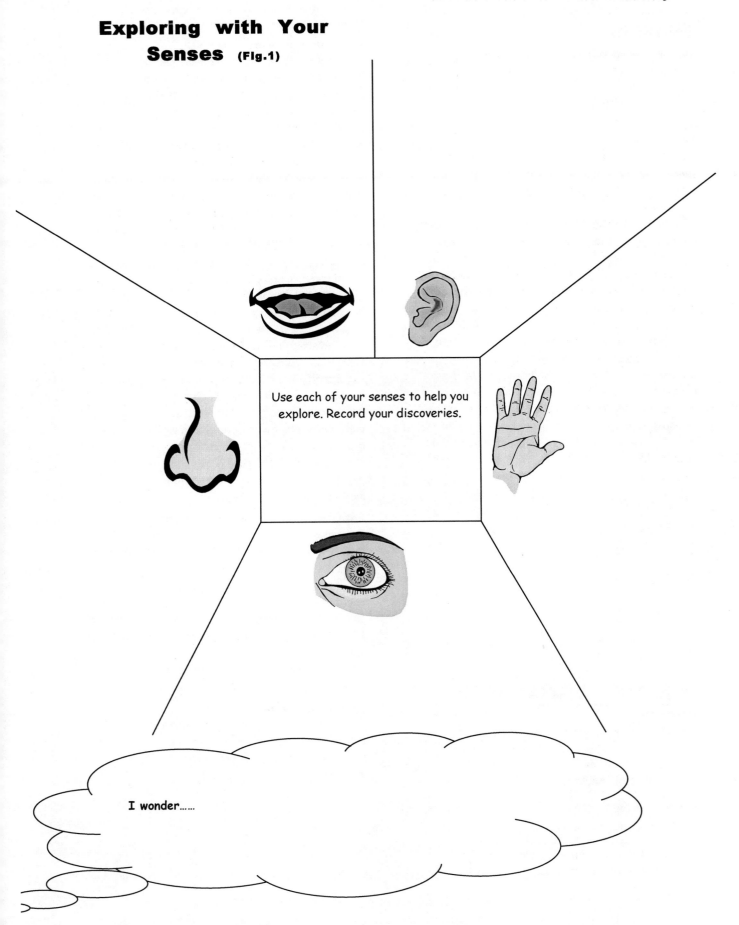

Use each of your senses to help you explore. Record your discoveries.

I wonder......

InfoSkill:

Define a Research Topic
Students will narrow or broaden a research topic to develop a personal focus for inquiry.

Skill Discussion

Finding just the right focus is crucial to the success of the research. If students are to 'buy in,' you need to build their curiosity and help them find relevance in the topic.

Students need sufficient background information on the topic so that they can identify the areas that hold intrigue for them. They also need to be immersed in activities that provide opportunity to explore the topic, link ideas to prior learning, and make personal connections. Once they have found an area of personal interest they need to define their research focus. If the focus is too narrow, gathering enough information to make it interesting and worthwhile will be difficult if not impossible. If the topic is too broad the amount of information available will be so vast that it will be unmanageable and will very likely become an "all about" project with little or no processing of data gathered.

Focus Your Topic		
What do I know?	What do I need to find out?	Where can I start searching?
Keywords and Key phrases		

Link Up

- Koechlin, C. and Zwaan, S. 1997. *Information Power Pack Junior Skillsbook*. Markham ON: Pembroke.
- Inspiration Software Inc.
  http://www.inspiration.com
- Brainstorming Techniques
  http://www.swc.utexas.edu
  /samples/writingprocess/brainstorm.pdf
- Internet Links for Narrowing the Topic of a Research Paper http://otel.uis.edu/
  yoder/narrowlitrev.htm

Novice: *Narrow to Categories*

Teach through Geography

Students are investigating ecozones of North America. Provide students with background exploratory experiences (*Explore a Topic* pg. 4) In large groups of five or six, instruct students to recall by brainstorming all they know about ecozones. Before commencing, review group work skills and rules for brainstorming. Provide students with a pile of sticky notes and instruct them to individually put one idea on each sticky. If the flow of ideas slows down remind them to close their eyes and think about some of the exploratory activities. An official spy could be appointed in each group and sent off to other groups to record fresh ideas to bring back to the group.

Ask each group to share and then continue brainstorming. Discuss with students how this will help everyone to think of more ideas and broaden their information on the topic. After a designated time, stop brainstorming and ask students to sort and classify their ideas on a large chart paper. The stickies make it very easy for students to shuffle ideas around. Using markers, name the categories e.g. rainforest, tundra etc. Share with other groups and note variety in categories. Discuss how they decided on the categories and how this process helps to break up a huge topic into narrower areas of focus.

Gathering Evidence of Understanding

Instruct students to decide on a category that they are really keen on exploring further. Provide them with the organizer *Target Your Topic Fig. 2* and have them record what they already **know** about it, what they **need** to discover, **where** they can go to find out about it, and some **keywords** they can use for successful searches. Students should be able to complete all sections with relevant information. Adequate keywords and phrases are key to successful searches.

Novice Adaptation

The sticky note activities are engaging for all learners, non-readers can often sketch their ideas. Post the charts around your classroom to build a word wall and extend vocabulary and ideas for all.

Apprentice: *Narrow to Categories and Sub-categories*

Teach through Science

A week or so before students are to start on an inquiry about insects start to build up their interest. Read great books about insects like *Ladybug Garden* by Celia Godkin. Watch video clips, and go an "insect walk" to take photos and video footage of insects in their natural habitat. Work in the school library to scan books and Internet sites. As students are exploring have them fill out fact cards with the name of the insect, a rough sketch, and basic information like size, habitat and diet. Students can make duplicates of their cards and trade with others during the exploration.

Keep a class chart of all the insects discovered by your young ornithologists. Ensure that there are resources to allow them to discover insects other than those in their own environment. e.g. fireflies, snow fleas... At a designated time conclude the exploration and form small groups of four students. Instruct students to lay out all their cards and sort them by similar characteristics. e.g. beetles, moths, insects that live in water, insects that bite etc. Share categories by group. Chart categories and discuss. Ask groups to shuffle their cards and regroup using different categories. Now have the students break down each category into sub-categories e.g. Beetles - flying, striped, spotted.

Gathering Evidence of Understanding

Discuss with students how this activity helped them to broaden their knowledge about insects and also how it helped them to narrow their focus to a manageable aspect of the topic. Develop with students a list of *Tips for Narrowing a Research Topic, Fig. 3.* Instruct students to use the *Target Your Topic, Fig. 2,* organizer to narrow their research topic. Students should be able to start from the broad topic of insects and narrow to categories and sub-categories to help them focus on a topic of interest.

Apprentice Adaptation

Groups could put their quick facts about insects in a simple database so they can create charts and graphs to demonstrate the kinds of insects their group discovered and later make links as they compare.

InfoStar: *Narrow Using Technology*

Teach through Guidance

Students are investigating future career opportunities. Working in pairs, instruct students to do subject searches in the online catalog and jot down related subject headings. Instruct students to explore specialized database and browse subject searches and "see also" references to give them ideas for breaking down the large topic.

Gathering Evidence of Understanding

Have students brainstorm and develop categories and sub-categories of career choices for their future. Use commercial software such as *Inspiration Software™* or a draw program for students to record and sort their ideas. Ask students to make an entry in their research journal reflecting on how this process helped them to broaden their thinking about future careers and how it helped to spark a topic for further, more focused, inquiry. Students should be able to make effective uses of search tools and software to help them work more efficiently.

Notes: Reflect, Rethink, Redesign

© Do students understand the connection between exploring the topic and developing a focus for research?
© Were there sufficient resources for all students to explore at the same time?
© Do students have enough background knowledge of the topic to develop a research focus?

Documenting the Evidence

Learner Level
Understanding of Skill:
© Brainstorms fluently.
© Develops appropriate categories and sub-categories.
© Defines a plausible, manageable focus for research.
Understanding Curriculum Content:
© Demonstrates accurate use of a broad range of content vocabulary.
© Makes appropriate connections to key concepts.

Target your Topic (Fig. 2)

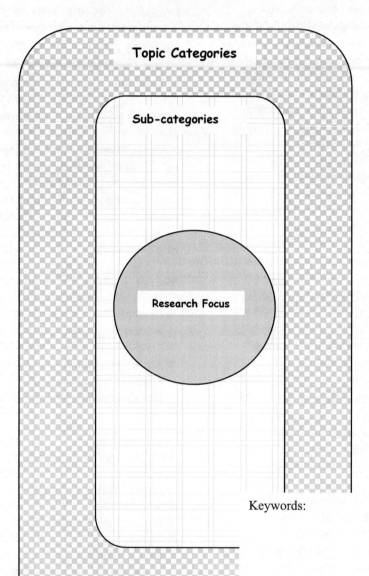

Broad Topic Brainstorming

Topic Categories

Sub-categories

Research Focus

Keywords:

Tips for Narrowing a Research Topic
(Fig. 3)

• Explore the broad topic - read, view, listen, talk.
• Ask questions.
• Jot down your thoughts.
• Make sketches and idea webs.
• Make connections to other things you know.

Narrowing a Topic

• Brainstorm what you already know about this topic.
• Sort your ideas into categories and sub-categories.
• Make groups of things, places, ideas, people...
• Breakdown into time frames, locations, events or stages.
• Think about causes, effects, opinions, arguments and spins on an issue.
• Free write questions that come to mind about the topic.
• Use *Topic Target* or develop your own organizer to help you narrow
   down the broad topic to something you are personally keen to research.

Broadening a Topic

• Consider other things, places, ideas, people...
• Expand the time frames, locations, events or stages.
• Explore causes, effects, opinions, arguments and spins on an issue.
• Make use of tables of contents, sub-headings and headings to
   discover larger context.
• Use online catalogs and databases to find related subjects.
• Scan "see also" links for related topics.
• Free write questions that come to mind about the topic.
• Use *Target Your Topic, Fig. 2,* or develop your own organizer to help you
   broaden your topic to something you are personally keen to research.

Examples

Narrowing a Topic

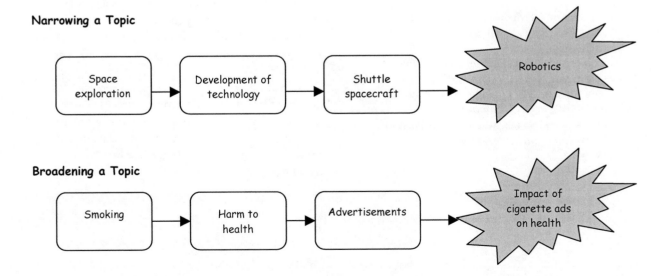

Broadening a Topic

InfoSkill:

Develop Questions
Students will develop effective questions to guide their research.

Skill Discussion

Research is the question. Successful research projects are dependant on the quality of the question(s). To be able to think critically about a topic, students need to develop effective questions to guide the research process. They need questions that drive analysis. Keep in mind that students cannot develop questions about a topic they have had no experience with. Part of the secret to developing good research questions is to provide students with rich exploratory experiences so they have something solid to hook their new learning to.

If students are thus stimulated, natural curiosity should take over. A flurry of questions will be generated. Helping students to become more conscious of the kinds of questions they formulate and helping them to realize which questions will generate high-level critical thinking is the next challenge.

Link Up

• Question Matrix: http://members.ozemail .com. au/~aslant/TheQuestionMatrix.doc
• Questioning Techniques for Gifted Students: http: //www.nexus.edu.au/teachstud/gat/painter.htm#top
• Questioning.org: http://questioning.org
• Learning Skills Program: Bloom's Taxonomy: http://www.coun.uvic.ca/learn/program/hndouts/bloom.html
• Bloom's Taxonomy's Model Questions and Key Words: http://www.utexas.edu/student/utlc/handouts/1414.html
• Morgan, Nora and Juliana Saxton. 1994. *Asking Better Questions: Models, Techniques and Classroom Activities for Engaging Students in Learning. Markham,ON: Pemboke.*
• Koechlin, Carol and Sandi Zwaan. 1997. *Teaching Tools for the Information Age.* Markham, ON. Pembroke.

Novice: *Model Questioning*

Teach Through Language

Become very knowledgeable about levels of questioning and techniques. Surround students with examples of effective questions.

• Daily discussion starters
• Prompts for learning logs
• Bulletin board displays to introduce new books
• Pre/during and post reading and viewing
• Developing surveys
• Planning for interviews
• Games such as Trivial Pursuit® , or Jeopardy®.
• Overarching questions based on learning outcomes to frame units of study (Wiggins and McTighe)

Gathering Evidence of Understanding

You will notice that students use questions more in their own writing. They should begin to realize that there are different kinds of questions for every purpose.

Apprentice: *Generate Questions Using a Question Matrix*

Teach Through Language

The class is working on a theme unit focusing on Leaving Home. Select a wonderful picture book such as *Gleam and Glow* by Eve Bunting or *My Grandfather's Journey* by Allen Say.
Show the cover and initiate discussion. Invite students to ask questions. Record the questions. Read to a climactic point in the story and ask for more questions. Record. Finish the story, review, and discuss recorded questions. Again ask for further questions. Record. Review all the generated questions for the purpose of learning more about different kinds of questions and their purposes. Clip questions from the chart and ask students to look for similarities. Organize in a large space. Cluster by question starter. (who, what, when, where, why and how) Instruct students to look at the second word. (is, are, were, would, will...)

Use a large wall space to sort and organize questions into a question matrix. Discuss which questions were easy to answer and why, which were more difficult and which questions had no direct answer in the story but are really interesting questions.

Gathering Evidence of Understanding

Provide each student with a question matrix template and an interesting photo or magazine picture. Instruct students to study the picture and formulate as many questions as they can. Students should experiment with question starters on the matrix. They should be able to form questions that can be directly answered from the photo as well as questions that require analysis, inferences and predictions.

Apprentice Adaptation

Younger students and beginning readers may need a physical aid to get them started. Make up a card for each of the starter phrases from the question matrix.

e.g. how are...

who will....

where is.....

when could .....

Have students develop questions orally. Learning buddies could help them record their questions.

InfoStar: *Generate Questions by Purpose*

Teach Through Career Studies

Ask students to think about careers that require good questioning skills. Instruct them to list careers and record why questioning is a vital skill for each career. Brainstorm in small groups and record ideas on a T-chart. Share group charts and display them.

Provide each group with a career scenario and ask students to generate 6-8 questions the person in this situation would probably need to ask. (e.g. A mechanic is talking to a car owner who hears a persistent but irregular rattle in his car.) Each group has a different scenario. When completed instruct three groups to move together and share questions. Have students discuss the kinds of questions asked then cluster and categorize similar questions. Groups share ideas and look for common elements in categories. Discuss and summarize discoveries made about questions.

Gathering Evidence of Understanding

Review common purposes for questions.

Questions that require:
- Factual answers
- Recall of events
- Clarification of ideas
- Organization of ideas
- Problem solving
- Some analysis of information
- Generation of new ideas
- Making decisions or evaluation

Instruct students to find examples of each kind of question and produce a chart of samples. Students should be able to find or write a sample question for each purpose.

InfoStar Adaptation

Work with students to develop a rubric for assessing effective research questions. Criteria for assessment might include:
- Focus/scope
- Evidence of need for higher level thinking
- Personal interest
- Application of knowledge

The purpose of this rubric would be to help student researchers diagnose the effectiveness of their questions and rework to design a great inquiry question to focus their efforts. Remember the question is the research.

Notes:
Reflect, Rethink, Redesign
- © Are students using focus words such as function, importance, survival, conditions, characteristics in their questions?
- © Are they including words to help them discover relationships? e.g. compare, cause, effect, significance, consequences...
- © How can I integrate the use of questioning skills in all curriculum areas?
- © Do improved questioning skills better focus the time spent on locating and selecting so that there is more time for processing information and developing understanding?

Documenting the Evidence

Learner Level
Understanding of Skill:
- © Understands the hierarchy of questions.
- © Realizes the power of good questions.

Student develop questions that:
- © Require more than a collection of facts.
- © Stimulate personal curiosity, enthusiasm.
- © Require comparison .
- © Direct personal reflection/opinion.
- © Promote analysis and synthesis of information.

Understanding Curriculum Content:
- © Analyzed information.
- © Synthesized information.

InfoSkill:
Keywords
Students will identify and use keywords to guide their searches for information.

Skill Discussion

Successful searches depend on the student's ability to develop a list of keywords and key phrases to guide their searches. Success with this skill is directly related to the amount of time invested in the explore stage. During this stage the students develop a related vocabulary and a working knowledge of the topic.

Keywords and phrases are very important because they relate directly to the universal ways information is classified and stored for retrieval. Even though information sources bear common elements each kind of resource has a different language and access structure.

Teach students how different kinds of information texts are organized. Teach them how the use of keywords will help them target the data they need. Student success depends on search strategy skills and development of a bank of keywords and key phrases.

> **Tips for expanding keywords/phrases**
> - Use a dictionary or thesaurus.
> - Look for synonyms/related terms.
> - Think of broader terms/concepts.
> - List associated names/ organizations.
> - Abbreviations/alternate spellings.
> - Review exploratory experiences.

Link Up

- Information Literacy Skills: Seeking
http://www.assd.winnipeg.mb.ca/infozone/seek.html
- Keyword searches
http://www.occ.act.edu.au/home/itpd/searching/keyword.htm
- Web Searches
http://teacher.scholastic.com/technology/tutor/websearch.htm
- Kidsclick
http://sunsite.berkeley.edu/KidsClick!/

Teach through History

The class is preparing to investigate the impact of the fur trading industry on the development of North America. Develop with students a list of information texts. Instruct students to examine a variety of print information texts. e.g. encyclopedia, non-fiction books, magazines, newspapers. Which features of these texts help us to find information we need? e.g. table of contents, index, headings, sub-headings, chunking and organizing information. These features help to zero in on what we need when we skim and scan.

If we know the keywords and phrases to look for we should be able to find exactly what we want and the search should be faster. This is especially true with electronic searches. Instruct student to think about the exploratory activities and then brainstorm together keywords and phrases that would be effective for this topic e.g. fur trade, courier de bois, explorers, beaver hat, North West Fur Company, American Fur Company, J.J.Astor.

Gathering Evidence of Understanding

Working in groups with samples of information texts instruct students to develop a chart which identifies the special search features each resource has to help them find information. Instruct students to test out the list of keywords to locate relevant information for this project Have them record their findings on the chart. Students should be able to scan/use the search features of the text to help them search by keyword efficiently.

Resource Title..

Search feature	Keyword/phrase	location
index	beaver, pelts	Pg. 26-28
table of contents	American Fur Company	Pg. 52 - 67

Novice Adaptation

Very young students can readily learn to use a table of contents and an index to find information, but developing keywords to guide searches is a complex process and needs to be modeled and developed with many experiences. Conference with students and provide keywords to help with searches. e.g. How do baby deer survive in the forest? (fawn, baby deer, food, mother, doe, habitat, home)

Apprentice: *Expand Keywords/phrases*

Teach through Science

Students are investigating the impact of space exploration on the quality of life. They have a good overview of the issues from their exploration, they have narrowed their topics and developed inquiry questions such as:

- How has space exploration advanced medicine?

Have students identify the key concepts in their question. (space exploration, advanced and medicine, medical benefits). Teach students how to expand the number of key- words by applying the tips for expanding key- words and phrases and the expansion chart These keywords or key phrases will be used in their searches.

Keyword/phrase Expansion Chart

Key Concepts	Expansion
"Space exploration"	"space industry" "space program" NASA space technology inventions
advanced	advancement helped contribution
medicine	health medical "medical discovery"

Gathering Evidence of Understanding

Instruct each student to create a keyword/phrase expansion chart. Have the students record their search plans (space and medicine) and keep a record of their searches. Ask students to determine which keyword combinations were most effective. Students should be able to evaluate what worked and what didn't in their searches.

Apprentice Adaptation

For younger students and those with special needs work through the expansion of keywords together.

Work on language activities to teach students how to think flexibly e.g. play word association games.

InfoStar: *Develop a Search Plan*

Teach through Dramatic Arts

Students are to research the history of a specific dramatic form and present their information in a creative timeline. e.g. mime, puppetry, mask making, storytelling

In preparing students for this assignment make use of their artistic talents. Use the activities of preparing for research and developing a search plan as an opportunity to think creatively. Urge students to really expand their repertoire of sources for information. Instruct them to develop a chart listing resources they plan to access and the keywords and phrases to guide their searches.

They will need to make some predictions or "educated guesses" about to how to find the information they need based on their knowledge and experiences. Encourage students to conference with each other and share strategies and ideas.

Gathering Evidence of Understanding

Students will prepare and implement a search plan and evaluate the results. Students should demonstrate flexibility and the ability to adjust and rework their plan as necessary.

Notes:
Reflect, Rethink, Redesign

◎ Are students hitting dead ends in their searches? If so are they going back to their keyword lists to find more words and phrase to try?
◎ Is there evidence that they had adequate prior experience with the topic?
◎ What else could I provide in terms of background building experiences?

Documenting the Evidence

Learner Level
Understanding of Skill:
◎ Identifies and collects lots of keywords.
◎ Experiments with keyword searches.
◎ Refreshes and adds to list of keywords when necessary.
◎ Compiles a bank of effective keywords and phrases to locate useful sources.

InfoSkill

Develop a Plan
Students will analyze the elements of the assignment, develop a plan and implement it.

Skill Discussion

Part of the anxiety that sometimes builds up for students, teachers and parents when information tasks are assigned lies in fuzzy task definition or misunderstandings regarding the parameters of the task.

Ultimately we want students to be able to independently analyze a task and develop a personal plan of action.

A Research Plan:
- Provides a learning map
- Keeps everything organized
- Keeps you on task
- Helps meet assessment criteria
- Chunks the process
- Sets target dates

Link Up

• California School Library Association. *From Library Skills to Information Literacy: a handbook for the 21s^t century.* Hi Willow 1997. San Jose California.

• The Research Cycle
http://optin.iserver.net/fromnow/dec99/rcycle.html

• Loertscher, D & Woolls, B. (2002) *Information Literacy: A review of the research.* 2ND ed. San Jose, CA: HiWillow Research.

Novice: Model the Process
Teach through Science

Start with an inquiry question e.g. How do Arctic animals adapt to survive in their environment?

Ask students what they will have to do to find answers to this question. List the ideas. Have students help you put the ideas in order starting with what they might do first. Now you have a step-by-step plan. Record the steps and target dates on a large chart to be displayed in the class so students can check their progress. Refer to the chart regularly as the students progress through the assignment. Review the meaning and importance of each step and check student progress.

Strategies for first experiences

© Ensure that students understand research as a process. (see *Understanding the Research Process pg. 2*)

© Make the task as authentic and real world as possible.

© Ensure that assessment criteria is discussed, posted and distributed.

© Provide research equipment. (clipboards, stickies, highlighters, clips)

© Establish times for research activities in the library.

© Provide students with research folder or portfolios or make them together.

© Provide students with checklists and contracts so they can monitor their own progress.

© Prepare a bulletin board of the research plan to keep track of class progress. (step ladder, barometer, tower, researchometer, Fig. 4)

© Use the language of inquiry so students learn to understand process terms.

© Negotiate realistic target dates but build in time for crisis points and serendipity.

© Send a letter home explaining the process and encouraging parents to discuss progress with their child.

© Conference regularly with each student in person and/or by e-mail.

Gathering Evidence of Understanding

Have students evaluate the effect of the class plan on completion of the assignment and revise the plan if necessary. Have students evaluate their own use of the plan and set goals for personal improvement. Students should be able to articulate that the plan was like a road map to guide them. They should also appreciate the efficiencies of staying on task and keeping organized

Adaptation

Have learning buddies (volunteers or older students) assist struggling readers with independent components of research such as browsing non-fiction books for information to answer their questions.

Apprentice: *Follow a Research Plan Independently*
Teach through Social Science

The students are beginning a research assignment in which they are asked to investigate causes of hunger in the world and suggest some possible strategies for addressing this global problem. Provide or develop with students a set of checklist prompts for students for each step of the process you are using, e.g.

Define and Clarify Information Needs
- Understand the assignment and assessment
- Develop an action plan
- Record assignment requirements and due dates
- Explore the topic
- Brainstorm for topic ideas
- Relate what you know to the topic
- Create an inquiry question
- Develop keywords
- Identify possible sources for needed information
- Develop a search plan...
- Conference and discuss progress

Discuss the implications of each stage and the possible need to loop back and redo certain stages. e.g. find new and different keywords if their searches are unsuccessful or revisit their sources and collect more data if what they have is insufficient. Develop with students target dates for different stages of completion. Have students mark off the steps as they progress. See sample research checklists *Research Log* Fig. 6, and *Research Success* Fig.5.

Gathering Evidence of Understanding

Ask students to use their checklist to explain their progress to a peer. This experience will not only help the student to understand his own learning but it also will provide him with an opportunity to test out ideas with others. Student should be able to articulate what they have accomplished and where they are headed next.

InfoStar: *Create a Research Plan*
Teach through Media Arts

Students have been asked to investigate a media artwork or production and analyze the impact it has on themselves and their community. This task will require complex levels of investigation and analysis. Students will need to select a media art piece and critique it from their own perspective. They will then need to examine the socio-economic impact on their community. Students will be totally responsible for the process as well as the final product. Establish, with students, criteria for a good research plan. See *Planning for Research* Fig. 7. Encourage students to design a visual organizer to represent their research plans. Instruct students to consult their plan throughout the process, and adapt and revise it as necessary.
Gathering Evidence of Understanding

Students should be able to develop a logical plan that addresses all the task expectations. The plan should provide a process map for the student to follow to achieve the task. All inquiry elements should be included from defining the task to evaluating the learning. The plan should provide time lines, points of reflection and conferencing. Have students self assess their plan and its implementation. Set goals for improvement.

Notes: Reflect, Rethink, Redesign

© Is there evidence that the students realize the importance of all the stages of research?
© Do students use their research plan?

Documenting the Evidence
Learner Level
Understanding of Skill
©includes all stages of the process
©includes timelines
©knows "what to do next"
©includes reflection and conferencing
©follows/adjusts the plan
©executes the plan effectively
©meets deadlines

Understanding of Content
© comprehensive analysis of the function of the media art work
© communication of the impact was creative and effective

Teaching Unit Level
© Compare levels of student success and comfort with and without use of a plan.
© Look for links between the plan, the process and the product.

Researchometer
(Fig. 4)

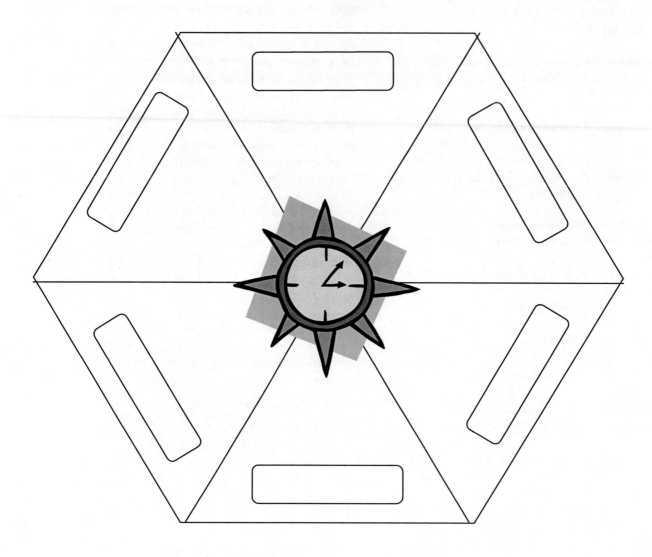

Use this visual organizer to plan and chart your research progress.

- Label major stages in each section
- Make a picture to illustrate each stage
     Or
- List things to do at each stage
- Record due dates for each stage
- Color or shade each section as you finish it
- Conference with a friend and/or your teacher at each stage
- Keep this researchometer in your research folder

 # Research Success
(Fig. 5)

What am I supposed to do?	How did I do?
Question and Wonder Explore the topic. Know what you need. Know where and how to look.	
Find and Sort Search books, videos, pictures, computer programs and people. Gather the best resources.	
Select and Record Find lots of good information. Make notes and sketches. Keep a source sheet. Put everything in a research folder.	
Think and Create Sort, classify and compare information. Use organizers to sort your notes. Talk about your discoveries.	
Summarize and Conclude Answer research problem. Make a summary, come to a conclusion, solve a problem or make a decision.	
Share New Ideas Decide how to share learning. Make a plan. Create something new and share it with others.	
Think about your work Think about how well you did. Talk to your teacher about what was good and what you need to work on. Think about why your research is important.	

Research Log
(Fig. 6)

My Research Plan

First To Define My Information Needs I:
- understand what I need to do
- know how it will be marked
- made a plan with due dates
- explored the topic
- recorded my inquiry question and subtopics
- have a list of keywords and phrases
- started a research folder

To Locate and Retrieve Resources I:
- searched our library online catalog, the bookmarked websites, the encyclopedia, etc.
- located lots of different kinds of resources
- skimmed text, content pages, titles, subtitles, pictures, sidebars
- checked to make sure I could understand it
- checked out the resources I need

To Select, Process and Record I:
- found data that meets my needs
- made point form notes and sketches
- put all my papers in my research folder
- kept a source sheet
- organized my data by subtopic
- checked to be sure I had enough, good data

To Analyze and Synthesize I:
- looked for connections
- looked for similarities and differences
- discovered what was fact and what was fiction
- organized, classified, categorized
- made a discovery
- came to a conclusion or asked a new question

To Share and Use My New Knowledge I:
- reviewed the task description
- decided on a sharing format
- made a sharing plan
- gathered things I need
- created the product/presentation
- practiced then shared my new ideas

To Reflect Transfer and Apply I:
- talked with my teacher about my research project (process and product)
- thought about what I did well, how I can do better
- reflected on how what I learned is important

Next time.....

My Research Log

Due Date...........................
Conference Notes:

Due Date...........................
Conference Notes:

Due Date...........................
Conference Notes:

Due date...........................
Conference Notes:

Due Date...........................
Conference Notes:

Due Date...........................
Conference Notes:

Planning for Research
(Fig. 7)

What is the purpose of your research?

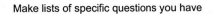

Brainstorm everything you know already	Make lists of specific questions you have

What do you think you will discover?

- Think about causes, consequences, impact and possible solutions.
- Think about relationships and perspectives, the big picture.

What do you think you will discover?

How will this assignment be assessed?

- What is important for you to do to be successful?
- How do due dates fit into your other workload
- and commitments?

How will this assignment be assessed?

Develop a plan of action

- Create a work flow chart, research cycle diagram or research map.
- What do you need to do and when will you have it finished?
- Who will you conference with along your research journey?
- How will you know you have been successful?
- Assess your work and set goals for improvement.

Develop a plan of action: Visual of Plan:

Notes:

Part 2: Locate and Retrieve

Once a clear focus for research has been defined, this hunting and gathering stage is usually very fruitful for all. Success in the research process will depend to a great extent on the relevance and appropriateness of the data the student uncovers. These tasks will help your students develop the skills necessary to locate and retrieve resources that are useful for their specific needs.

(p24) Use Search Strategies
Novice: Search OPAC Using Prompts
Apprentice: Search Online Databases
InfoStar: Search the Internet

(p28) Locate Resources
Novice: Limited Locations
Apprentice: Multiple Locations
InfoStar: School Library and Beyond

(p32) Skim, Scan and Consider
Novice: For Personal Interest
Apprentice: For Information Need
InfoStar: For Analysis of Information

(p34) Evaluate Resources
Novice: Student Need Personal Criteria
Apprentice: Given Criteria and Tool
InfoStar: Student Created Criteria and Tool

(p40) Design Surveys
Novice: Teacher Directed
Apprentice: Collaborative Development
InfoStar: Independent

(p46) Use Primary Sources
Novice: Collect Artifacts
Apprentice: Conduct Interviews
InfoStar: Gather Virtual Resources

InfoSkill:

Search Strategies
Students will use search strategies effectively to locate electronic resources.

Skill Discussion

Surfing the net is usually not a productive strategy for students. As the Cheshire Puss told Alice when you don't know where you are going any road will take you there. We need to teach students to determine their destination and map their journey thoughtfully. The sheer volume of information available drives the need for students to approach use of the Internet strategically.

Teachers and library media specialists must work together to carefully design and scaffold programs that require students to make effective use of electronic information, particularly the Internet. Students must be able to both determine their direction and read the signposts along the way.

Online Search Plan, Fig. 9

Online Search Plan

Information focus/inquiry question

Possible keywords/search phrases

Information Need:
(types of information)

This search would be best using:
(sources)

Link Up
- Noodle Tools http://www.noodletools.com/
- Effective Search Strategies Kathy Schrock http://school.discovery.com/schrockguide/searching/
- Jupiter Research Web Searching Tips http://searchenginewatch.com/facts/
- Evaluating Internet Resources http://eduscapes.com/tap/topic32.htm

Novice: *Search OPAC Using Prompts*

Teach Through Science

Students are investigating the interdependence of plants and animals in specific habitats. They have each selected a habitat they are curious about and have developed their questions to guide the research. They need to begin locating suitable resources by searching the school library OPAC.

As a class, review and list search strategies. Develop some prompts to guide the students as they search. Use these prompts to create visuals, e.g., a poster beside the computers, index cards taped to computer desks or perhaps standing in inexpensive clear plastic photo displays beside the computer.

Smart Search Strategies
© Identify your information need - question/focus statement
© Brainstorm for keywords
© Look for synonyms or related terms (use a thesaurus)
© Use proper names (use caps e.g. Leonardo Di Caprio)
© Narrow or broaden search (e.g. dogs, canine)
© Use Boolean searching(e.g. and, or not)
© Test your search
© Scan results
© Revise search using different keywords if necessary

Model the skills of developing keywords, (see pg 14-15) and applying search strategies. Teach students how to find full descriptions of "hits" in your library holdings and discuss how they could decide which "hits" might be suitable for their research. Remind students to keep reviewing their research questions or focus.

Gathering Evidence of Understanding

Provide students with the organizer, *My Best Hits* Fig. 8. Instruct students to complete the box *Preparing for Searching,* on the organizer and then work in pairs at the library catalog to search for and record the names and call numbers of suitable resources. When they have done this, students should be able to go to the stacks and find the titles by call number. They should browse through each resource to make sure it meets their needs and then check out the best resources and begin their investigation, or revise their search strategies and try again if they have not been successful.

Students should list the search strategies they used, comment on which were the most successful and explain why they think those strategies worked.

Adaptation

Depending on the number of computers you have available for this activity you may want to rotate students through these activities as others begin searches in print and online encyclopedias, videos, and selected Internet sites.

Apprentice: *Search Online Databases*

Teach through Geography

Students have a focused assignment on the changing patterns in world population growth. They are going to begin their searches in on-line encyclopedias and periodical databases. Review *Smart Search Strategies* (p. 24) and demo a related search. Highlight all the special features that the online databases have to make finding and using information effective and efficient for users.
• Search tools
• Hyperlink article contents
• Hyperlink text in the body of the article
• Subject directories
• Charts and maps
• Multimedia
• Links to web sites
• Links to periodical articles
• Citation information
• Saving and printing features

Gathering Evidence of Understanding

Observe students as they are working. Students should be able to identify which special text features they used and explain their effectiveness.

InfoStar: *Search the Internet*

Teach Through Information Technology

Teach students how search engines, metasearch engines, and directories, work and how they are developed. Demonstrate how to use them and discuss the best uses, advantages, and disadvantages of each search tool. Provide students with lots of practice, discovering for themselves, the best search engines and directories for specific purposes. Set up search scenarios for small groups of students. Discuss results.

Gathering Evidence of Understanding

Provide students with the organizer *Online Search Plan, Fig. 9,* and have them complete it as they search. They should be able to identify search tools by name and explain their purpose. Have students asterisk the searches that were most successful.

Instruct them to keep multiple copies of *On-line Search Plan* in their research folder so they will always have one ready when they are preparing to search online.

Adaptation

Teach students how to develop a favorites file on their home computer desktop or save to a disk or personal file for school access.

Notes:
Reflect, Rethink, Redesign

© Are there students who are experiencing a low "hit rate"?
© Which students are having difficulty?
© Is insufficient content knowledge impairing the development of successful search terminology?
© How can I quickly and effectively provide background information to familiarize students with the language of the topic?
© What other reasons could there be for failure?

Documenting the Evidence

Learner Level
Understanding of Skill
© selects useful keywords
© selects appropriate search strategies
© applies appropriate search strategies
© identifies specific search engines for selected purposes
© locates useful information
Understanding of Curriculum Content
© acquires relevant information from a variety of sources

Organization Level
© resources available for students of all levels
© adequate resources
© adequate hardware
© multiple access points

My Best Hits

(Fig. 8)

Preparing for Searching
Name:...My topic:...............................
I wonder..
....
Keywords to help my search............................ ....
....
....

- Search your library catalog for resources to help with your investigation.
- Remember you should use books, CD-ROMs, and videos to look for information.
- If you get stuck ask your library media specialist or your learning buddy for help.
- Read the notes to decide if the resource is good for you.

Keyword.................................# hits........................
Title...call #...................
Title...call #...................

Keyword.................................# hits........................
Title...call #...................
Title...call #...................

Keyword.................................# hits........................
Title...call #...................
Title...call #...................

- I also found a story book about my topic that I would like to read.
  Title...call #...................
- Go and look for these books on the shelves. Ask for help if you cannot find them yourself.
- Look inside each book and read a little bit. Pick the best two books for your research and check them out.

Online Search Plan
(Fig. 9)

Name:..**Topic:**..

Information focus/inquiry question ....

....

....

Possible keywords/search phrases ....

....

....

Information Need

• Quick facts • Statistics • Maps • Primary sources • Multimedia • Biographical information • Government sites • News coverage • Perspectives on an issue • Historical data •	• Explore a topic • Authoritative information • "How to" information • Shopping • Entertainment • Travel • Education • Weather •

Think about the best **search tools** to address your information need. Remember a **search engine** sources and links Web pages by machine. Use a search engine when you know the information is there e.g. places, organizations, and people. Web pages in a directory are sourced and linked by people. Use a **directory** (a list of websites someone is recommending) to explore a topic and to source academic information. Use **periodical databases** to discover perspectives on issues. **Online Encyclopedias** are often reliable starting points for research and often have good links to selected Websites and periodicals

This search would be best using:

- Online Encyclopedia..
- Directory..
- Periodical database..
- Search Engine..

Assessment of results:

InfoSkill:
Locate Resources
Students will locate resources relevant to their defined need.

Skill Discussion

Students need to be familiar and comfortable with the layout of the school library media center. Access to the LMC must be inviting and it must be open for students at all times. Students must know where different types of material are located and how to access the specific resources they need for their inquiries and interests. Students who are proficient at locating resources are able to devote more time to selecting and processing the data they need. We need to design meaningful activities in the context of current curriculum to facilitate development of locating skills.

Tips

Make *browsing cards,* about 4"x18", from bristol board. Or obtain new paint stir sticks from a local paint dealer. Train students to slip one in the space between books that would be left when they remove a book from the shelf to check it for relevance to their need. These placeholders indicate exactly where to replace rejected books and can save hours in shelving and sorting.

Link Up

- Location skills are best taught in the context of a purposeful curriculum task. The need must be real. These links will help you with tools and strategies that can be adapted and integrated to suit your curriculum application.

- Taylor, Paige, Brinkmyer Sue and Kent. (2001) *Dewey & the Decimals: learning games & activities.* Wisconsin: Alleyside Press.

- Dewey Browse
  http://www.deweybrowse.org/

- How to Use the Dewey Decimal System
  http://www.monroe.lib.in.us/childrens/ddchow.html

Novice: *Limited Locations*

Teach Through Language Arts

Students are asked to locate picture books of a certain author. Read the class a story written by a popular author. Ask students if they know other books by this author. If possible show a picture and discuss some of the author's life history. Show the students a number of books by the author and ask them to examine the outside of the books to discover things that are the same. (e.g. name of author, perhaps illustrator and publisher and spine label) Examine other books for spine labels and help students discover the purpose of spine labels.

Give each student a scavenger card (preferably on a topic being studied) with the call number of a picture book. Have students locate a book by matching their scavenger card to spine labels. Students read the book until the teacher is able to check their selection. Often students will want to sign out the book. If not, provide another card.

E McD	E McD Jabuti the Tortoise
F KRO The Countess & Me	811.54 Bou Voices from Wild An Animal Sensagoria

Gathering Evidence of Understanding

Students should be able to use the clues on the scavenger card to help them locate the book. Eventually students should be able to use call numbers to locate their favorite authors or series in many locations. Students having difficulty may need a learning buddy.

Adaptation

With very young children you may have them locate books by only the first letter of the author's name. Proceed to author and title scavenger cards, as students are ready. Use this strategy to introduce other sections of the collection, as students are ready.

Apprentice: *Multiple Locations*

Teach Through Science

Create scavenger hunts to use during the exploration stage of research. As part of the preparation for a study of animal classification, organize students into home groups and assign an animal type to each group. (e.g. reptiles) Record the call numbers and titles of lots of relevant resources, each on separate index cards, and give a stack of scavenger cards, related to the assigned animal type, to each group. Include every kind of resource possible. e.g. magazines, reference, kits, and videos. Individually, students locate a resource, mark the spot with a *browsing card*, and bring the resource back to the home group. Students skim and scan the item and find something special about the resource to share with the home group.

Gathering Evidence of Understanding

Students return the resource back to the correct location and retrieve their browsing card. Scavenger cards for reptiles are placed back on the table and the groups rotate and begin again with another animal type (e.g. mammals). Continue rotation as time permits.
After a couple of rotations you should observe that students are locating resources by call number quite efficiently.

InfoStar: *School Library and Beyond*

Teach Through Geography

After introducing the topic of "energy sources", have students work in groups to brainstorm the kinds of resources they may need to begin their exploration of this topic. Have each group fold a paper in half to create a T-CHART. On one side instruct students to list general resources and on the other side note where or how they could locate them.

Resource	Location
Online encyclopedia	school library computer school lab computers public library computer home computer

Encourage students to seek out community resources, agencies and organizations that could provide information for this topic. Remind students that as well as books and Internet sites there are many other ways to locate information. They can e-mail, FAX, write a letter, make a telephone call, conduct an interview do a poll or visit a specialized display. Provide students with *Resource Check, Fig. 10,* to prompt them to expand their search area.

Gathering Evidence of Understanding

When students have explored their topic and formulated questions and keywords to guide their searches, instruct them to locate the best resources to meet their information need. Students should be able to demonstrate that they not only know where to find resources to support their investigation but they also know how and when some resources will be better for their need than others. Provide students with source sheets (e.g. Log of Sources, Fig. 11) so they can record all the information they require should they need to access them again for further information.

Notes:
Reflect, Rethink, Redesign

© Do students require a review of Dewey Decimal Classification?
© Did I include some unusual and interesting books for scavenger cards to make it more fun? e.g. insects: walking sticks, cockroaches, fireflies, snow fleas...
© Can I adapt the Scavenger Hunt to a history topic by providing clues leading students to locate information on specific social and cultural aspects of an era?
© Where else can I use this strategy?

Documenting the Evidence

Organization Level
© materials are in shelf list order
© sections and shelves are well labeled
© resources are adequate in number and variety
© layout is logical
© materials are easily accessible
© layout accommodates ease of supervision

Resource Check
(Fig. 10)

Use this page or make up your own checklist to keep track of resources and tools you have used to gather the information you need.

Things I have consulted
- library catalog (OPAC)
- print encyclopedias
- online encyclopedia
- non-fiction books
- specialized reference books
- internet
- online periodical database
- CD-ROM
- video
- television program
- magazine
- newspaper
- atlas
- almanac
- charts and posters
- pamphlets
- telephone book
- dictionary
- thesaurus
-

Places I have visited
- school library
- public library
- reference library
- environmental organization
- museum
- art gallery
- government office
- historical site
- newspaper
-

Things I have done
- read
- viewed
- listened
- talked
- searched
- surveyed
- interviewed
- written
- sketched
- faxed
- e-mailed
- brainstormed
- questioned
- scanned headings and visuals
- skimmed for relevant data
- kept good notes
- used graphic organizers
- created graphic organizers
- recorded all sources
-

People I have talked to
- teachers
- library media specialists
- reference librarian
- family
- friends
- community members
- experts on my topic
- politician
- environmental group
-

Next time....

Adapted from *Information Power Pack Junior Skillsbook*, Pembroke Publishers 1997.

Log of Sources (Fig. 11)

Record only the sources you found and used for your project. This list will help you find the resources again if you need to. It will also help you to make a formal Reference List if it is required for your assignment. Record all sources of information, print, digital and human.

Tip: Make use of the resource # to help you quickly link quotes and references e.g. notes, organizers, mind maps, and sticky notes.

Resource #	Type of Resource Call#	Resource data	Pages Used
1.		Title:.. Author(s):.. Publisher:.. Place of Publication...........................©....................	
2.		Title:.. Author(s):.. Publisher:.. Place of Publication...........................©....................	
3.		Title:.. Author(s):.. Publisher:.. Place of Publication...........................©....................	
4.		Title:.. Author(s):.. Publisher:.. Place of Publication...........................©....................	
5.		Title:.. Author(s):.. Publisher:.. Place of Publication...........................©....................	
6.		Web Site:.. Author(s):.. URL......:... Title of section.........................Last Updated...........	
7.		Web Site:.. Author(s):.. URL......:... Title of section.........................Last Updated...........	
8.		Web Site:.. Author(s):.. URL......:... Title of section.........................Last Updated...........	
9.		Web Site:.. Author(s):.. URL......:... Title of section.........................Last Updated...........	
10		Other..	

InfoSkill

Skim, Scan, Consider
Students will skim and scan resources to consider which information is relevant to their information need.

Skill Discussion

Skim and scan are old information skills that have not only stood the test of time but have become increasingly more important as the volume of data available explodes. This pre- reading skill set is a vital prerequisite for using information texts. We have added the evaluative component, "consider," linking the physical access of information to a cognitive activity. When these skills are presented and practiced in relevant and purposeful experiences they will have more meaning for students. Skim, scan, and consider must become a natural pre-reading strategy for all information tasks.

Skim for an overview by looking at the title, sub-titles, sidebars, bolded text, visuals, captions, first and last sentence on a page.

Scan for a specific piece of information such as a name, telephone number, URL or date or fact from print or visual text.

Consider the suitability of the resource to meet your need. Consider: readability, interest, currency, relevance and validity

Link Up

- Skim and Scan Reading
  http://www.nortcoll.ac.uk/skim_and_scan.htm

- Reading Strategies
  http://elearn.mtsac.edu/amla/54/rdstrats.htm

- Beers, Karlene. *No Time, No Interest, No Way* Pt.2 (1996). School Library Journal.

Novice: *For Personal Need*

Teach through Language Arts

This activity will provide an opportunity to introduce students to skimming and scanning as well as add some variety to your booktalk "menu". Ask students how they go about selecting a novel for pleasure reading. Chart the criteria they suggest. Teach and model the terms **skim** and **scan**. Examine the criteria students provided for selecting a book. Ask students to think about which pre-reading skills they are applying when they preview a book. Sort the criteria suggested by students for their personal book selection. Your chart will look something like this.

Skim for	Scan for
Title	Characters
Author	Setting
Cover visual	Rating
Reviews	Copyright date
Author bio	Connections
Synopsis	Genre /Storyline

Gathering Evidence of Understanding

Prepare a festive table (thematic if you wish) complete with tablecloth and candelabra. Fill large plastic bowls and baskets with lots of excellent reads to suit the range of skills and interests of your class. Invite students to sample the "book buffet" by applying their skimming and scanning skills to **consider** a book for pleasure reading. When students have found a book they want to devour they sit down and begin to read. If after scanning a few pages they are not hooked they return the book, select another, and continue sampling until they find the "just right" book for them. Observe students as they skim and scan the covers and consider their reading choices. They should be skimming the cover for a general overview of the book and scanning a few pages to discover details about the storyline. Before students check out their books debrief and ask students how their new skills helped them make choices.

Adaptation

Maintain an evolving list of student experiences using the skim, scan, and consider. e.g. using a phone book, selecting a magazine, checking recipes for food ingredients, comparing prices when shopping, using a TV guide etc.

The Book Buffet, skim, scan, consider approach may not motivate reluctant readers, so we need to vary book talks and other motivational reading activities to include non-fiction. Invite the reluctant readers to Movie Club to see the film adaptation of a book before they reading it. Show it to avid readers later and ask them to compare the two versions.

Apprentice: *For Information Need*

Teach through Social Science

Current material is needed for students to explore the factors that affect the development of children in today's society.

On a daily basis, provide students with current print newspapers and magazines. Instruct them to skim news article titles and photographs for articles on issues that impact children. Students then scan the article for details and consider if this article discusses issues related to child development. They then clip the desired articles and collect them in a file folder. After a few days have students meet in groups to share and discuss their clipping files. Students will then sort their articles looking for common themes. Have students name each category e.g. safety, nutrition, sports, education, parenting, television, etc. They are now ready to begin their inquiry with real world data.

Gathering Evidence of Understanding

Observe students as they work. They should be able to quickly skim periodicals to locate possible article, then scan the article for confirming details as they consider its relevance to their project. During sharing students should know enough about their article to predict the content and thus work with others to sort the articles into themes.

InfoStar: *For Analysis of Information*

Teach through Careers

Students are working collaboratively to begin building a career exploration webpage to be linked to the school library webpage as a resource for others. Review the skim, scan, and consider, skills before students begin searching. Students will work in partners to find and evaluate the best sites for specific careers. Instruct students to develop a search plan such as *Online Search Plan, Fig. 9,* and an evaluation tool similar to *Website Analysis, Fig. 13,* for validating websites.

Gathering Evidence of Understanding

Students will be demonstrating their ability to work their way through a lot of information effectively. To search efficiently they should skim the site for an overview and scan for details regarding authorship, copyright, intent, and context and as they consider and validate each site that they select for the webpage. Observe students as they work. Conference with each team during their searches and assess their search plan and their methods of analyzing the sites they are reviewing. Have teams review each other's sites before mounting on the web page.

Notes:
Reflect, Rethink, Redesign

© Was I able to help students see the personal benefits of mastering these skills?

© Does the ongoing graffiti chart, on which students record situations where they applied skim and scan, and consider, help them see the relevance of these skills?

© Did they note discoveries or make comments in their journals that I should ask them to share with the class or that I could incorporate in future lessons?

© Which students are having difficulty with these skills? Would a reading buddy help? What else can I do to support them?

Documenting the Evidence

Learner Level
Understanding of Skill
© skims when an overview is needed
© skims title, sub-titles, sidebars, bolded text, visuals, captions, first and last sentence
© scans when searching for a specific piece of information
© considers how findings relate to purpose or information need
© applies skills without prompting
© identifies data relevant to need

InfoSkill:

Evaluate Resources
Students will evaluate resources for usefulness.

Skill Discussion

Info-glut is a major problem for young researches. Determining whether or not resources are useful and reliable sources of information is a critical step when dealing with volumes of data. Students must first develop an awareness of their information need and then scan the text for evidence of relevance. They must also learn how to validate a resource by checking the contents against determined criteria. They need to realize that not everything they read, hear, and view, is reliable. The fact that it is produced in some way doesn't necessarily make it accurate or reliable. Students need strategies for examining information sources critically and lots and lots of practice applying them. Eventually evaluation of recreational reading material and information resources will become a natural step in their selection process.

Link Up

- Kathy Schrock's Guide for Educators: Critical Evaluation Information
  http://school.discovery.com/schrockguide/eval.html

- The Good the Bad and the Ugly
  http://lib.nmsu.edu/instruction/eval.html

- Knowing What's What and What's Not: the 5 W's (and 1 "H") of Cyberspace
  http://www.mediaawareness.ca/eng/webaware/tipsheets/w5.htm

- How to Critically Analyze Information Sources
  http://www.library.cornell.edu/okuref/research/skill26.htm

- Evaluating Web Pages: A WebQuest
  http://mciunix.mciu.k12.pa.us/~spjvweb/evalwebteach.html

Novice: *Student Need - Personal Criteria*

Teach through Language Arts

Read a picture book such as *Gifts* by Jo Ellen Bogart and Barbara Reid. Ask students to think about how they select a gift for a friend. *What does my friend like to do? How much can I spend? What is popular? How much time do I have to find something?*

Brainstorm information sources that would help find a special gift for a friend e.g. current catalogs, flyers, websites advertisements, window-shopping, consulting a friend. Develop an analogy: Shopping for a gift for a friend is like searching for the best books and information sources. Develop a list of questions students should ask themselves when looking for books and information.

Looking for a good book

What are your friends reading?
Do you have a favorite author or series?
Do you like to read mysteries, science fiction, fantasy poetry, adventure, how to....?
Do you like humorous or serious books?
What has your librarian recommended?

Looking for information

Do you need quick facts?
What is your research question?
What are your keywords?
Do you need very current information?
Are you looking for a particular perspective?

Gathering Evidence of Understanding

Provide students with copies of "Book Check" bookmarks from Fig. 12 to use when they visit the library media center. Have them complete the check boxes as they browse for the books and information they need. Talk to students as they search. They should be able to tell you what they need and how they will know it is a good resource for them. They should use the checkboxes on the bookmarks to help them decide if they have found the best resource for their need. Leave new Book Checks at the circulation desk for students to use on future visits.

Adaptation

Encourage younger students to sit down with their selected book and browse through it to make sure it is the best book for them.

Apprentice: *Given Criteria and Tool*

Teach through Civics

Students are preparing to investigate the structure and function of components of local, regional and national government bodies. Discuss why careful analysis of resources for this task is important. Provide small student groups with a variety of non-fiction resources to support this topic. e.g. Non-fiction books, magazines, pamphlets, videos and Internet sites. Ask students to explore these resources and determine how to find out if these resources will be good for their investigations. Where do you look, what do you do? e.g. skim for readability, find copyright date, read the review/synopsis on the back cover, determine author's credibility, etc.

Provide students with clues for analyzing the anatomy of a URL address.

Government sites	.gov
Education	.edu
Commercial sites	.com
Non-profit organizations	.org
Military	.mil
Countries	.us, .ca, .au, etc.

Debrief and develop criteria for evaluating usefulness of resources. Teach students to examine resources for credibility, accuracy, intent, context and perspective.

Gathering Evidence of Understanding

Instruct students to evaluate a resource they are considering as a source for their research. Use the organizer *Examine and Evaluate, Fig. 14,* or *Web Site Analysis, Fig. 13.* After completing the organizer students should be able to make an accurate decision about the usefulness of the resource.

InfoStar: *Student Developed Criteria and Tool*

Teach through Physical Education

Students are preparing to work in groups to investigate issues in competitive sports e.g. gender equality, doping, adjudication, sponsors, media coverage etc. Guide students to think critically about the nature and credibility of the resources that they will need to gather so they can address these issues from all relevant perspectives. Each group will be required to develop a plan for gathering and evaluating their sources. Groups will present their findings in elective seminars at an in-school conference.

Gathering Evidence of Understanding

As a component of their assignment assessment, each team will present their search plan and the evaluation tool(s) used for validating their sources. Students should keep a record of the resources they considered, including those they rejected, and be prepared to explain the reasons for their decisions.

Notes:
Reflect, Rethink, Redesign

© Do students understand the importance of validating resources?
© Has the quality of resources selected improved?
© Are students having difficulty locating quality information?
© Are students able to find the variety of perspectives needed?

Documenting the Evidence

Organization Level

Analyze collection, within a topic, for
© currency
© relevant perspectives
© reading levels
© variety of types of resources

Filling the gaps:
© utilize online databases and good websites
© find and study reviews and recommendations
© develop a wish list and prioritize
© prepare a budget proposal and lobby for funds
© collaborate and share resources with other libraries

Notes:

Book Check

Are you just browsing?

- ☐ Have you checked out a magazine lately?
- ☐ What about a joke book?
- ☐ Find books of puzzles and games.
- ☐ Do you like reading about famous people?
- ☐ Think about other things you are interested in e.g. sports, cooking, fashion, mysterious events etc.
- ☐ Search your library catalog for a topic of interest.
- ☐ Check out the "New Book" display.
- ☐ Ask friends what they have read.
- ☐ Ask your teacher-librarian for help
- ☐ **Found a keeper? Check it out!**

Book Check

Are you looking for a novel?

- ☐ Do you know the author/illustrator?
- ☐ Read reviews/synopsis on the back cover.
- ☐ Read book jacket flaps.
- ☐ Does the genre interest you?
  - ☐ Mystery
  - ☐ Adventure
  - ☐ Fantasy
  - ☐ Science fiction
  - ☐ Historical fiction
  - ☐ Contemporary
  - ☐
- ☐ Read the first paragraph to check interest.
- ☐ Skim a few pages for readability.
- ☐ Too difficult/easy or not interested? Try another book.
- ☐ **Looks great? Check it out!**

Book Check

Looking for quick Facts?

- ☐ Dates
- ☐ Statistics
- ☐ Places
- ☐ People

Try

- ☐ Atlas
- ☐ Almanac
- ☐ Encyclopedia
- ☐ Yearbooks

Need something for a project?

- ☐ Search catalog using keywords.
- ☐ Check table of contents and index for your keywords.
- ☐ Skim for headings, sub-headings and captions.
- ☐ Check for illustrations, charts, maps and other visuals related to your research need.
- ☐ Too difficult/easy or not interested? Try another book.
- ☐ **Perfect? Check it out!**

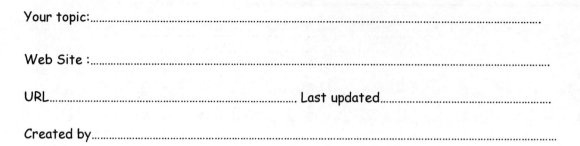

Web Site Analysis (Fig. 13)

Your topic:...

Web Site :...

URL.. Last updated...

Created by...

Evaluate this web site based on the following questions.

❑ Are there links to other good sites and/or related resources?

❑ Is the site attractive and inviting?

❑ Is the site at a good reading level for you?

❑ Are there useful special features like maps, charts, videos, and sound?

❑ Is the content easily searchable by subject or keyword?

❑ Is the site free of obvious bias?

❑ What do we know about the author to suggest he's and expert on the topic?

Bottom Line

Will this site be useful for your project?

Why? Or Why not?

Examine and Evaluate (Fig. 14)

Title:..
Author...
Publisher:...

What is your research question? What kind of information do you need?	
Validation Criteria	**Notes**
Accuracy • Up to date? • Statistical data/facts? • Opinions?	
Authority How credible is the writer/producer? • Qualifications? • Experience? Who financed the work? • Corporation? • Government agency? • Special interest group?	
Perspective Whose perspective is included? Whose voice is excluded?	
Slant/Intent What is the purpose? • Inform? • Convince? • Entertain? • Question? • Support?	
Context What is the context of the piece? • Historical? • Political? • Environmental? • Social? • Fiction? • Factual?	
Evidence of Bias • Exaggeration? • Prejudice? • Inclusion/exclusion? • Charged words? • Overgeneralization? • Opinion asserted as fact?	
Bottom Line Will this resource be useful for your project? Why? Why not?	

Adapted from *InfoTasks for Successful Learning*, Pembroke Publishers 2001

InfoSkill:

Design Surveys
Students will design surveys to collect primary data.

Skill Discussion

On some occasions the information students require is best gathered by means of a survey. This ensures that the data are current and, if the survey is well composed, relevant to the exact needs of the researcher. Surveying involves many skills, such as questioning, predicting, analyzing and managing time. These prerequisite skills must be taught or revisited. Although this is a highly engaging research strategy, student success depends on careful structuring of the process. Gather lots of surveys and have students analyze them for format, style and purpose. Teach survey etiquette and develop safety guidelines. Have students also try conducting surveys by telephone, FAX, mail, email, interview, and the Internet.

Link Up

- Media Awareness Network
  http://www.media-awareness.ca/

- Kathy Shrock's Critical Evaluation Surveys
  http://school.discovery.com/schrockguide/eval.html

- Questionnaires and Survey Design
  http://www.statpac.com/surveys/index.htm#toc

Teach Through Mathematics/Health

In health students need to discover the levels of participation in physical fitness activities in their community. They also need to gather data for input into a simple spreadsheet in a mathematics assignment. Discuss their data need. Together create a statement describing the purpose of the survey and explaining how the information will be used. Have the class brainstorm and record a list of the kinds of fitness activities available in their community. e.g. tennis, swimming, bowling, etc. Discuss criteria students may need to consider as they design their survey. Which ages will they target? Will they need to cluster age groups? Are they planning to break down the analysis between male and female? Is it important to know if the activity is free or whether there is a fee? Does it require special equipment? How often is the activity available? Remind students to ask only for information that is important to their purpose, making the questions specific so that answers are useful.

With students, decide on the types of questions that will be asked: Yes and No, True and False, Agree and Disagree based on a scale of 1 -5, short answer, cloze, etc. Once these kinds of decisions have been made, discuss the format and structure of the survey and develop a template with the students. Have students work with a partner to rehearse introductions, stating the purpose, conducting the survey and thanking the interviewee. Provide written instructions for students in the form of a checklist reminding students of proper etiquette, safety rules, timelines and appropriate targets for the survey.

Gathering Evidence of Understanding

Along with a clipboard, provide copies of the survey, a process checklist, and a letter explaining the purpose of the survey and telling how the data will be used. Students work in pairs taking turns conducting the survey. Together they should be able to collect the data needed for the mathematics spreadsheet lesson. The analysis of that data is interpreted for the health lessons.

See *Interpreting and Evaluating Graphs and Charts, Fig. 16.*

Adaptation

Very young children or second language learners may need the assistance of a learning buddy. They should begin with a simple survey of only 3 or 4 questions.

Apprentice: *Collaborative Development*

Teach Through Science

As part of an investigation of conservation of energy, students need to investigate primary data about recycling in their community. Collect different samples of surveys and copy enough so groups have a variety to examine. In small groups instruct students to look for common elements of surveys as well as differences in the kinds and levels of questions they discovered (e.g. fill in the blank, multiple choice, ranking, short answer and open-ended questions). As a class, discuss the kinds of information they are hoping to gather, groups they will target, types of questions and organizations that would best provide the information needed about recycling. Use the tips included in *Creating a Survey Action Plan, Fig. 17,* as a guide for the process.

Gathering Evidence of Understanding

Instruct students to work in groups to create a survey applying all the points and strategies discussed in the lesson. Make copies of the survey for each group member. Have each student make some predictions about the kind of information they think they will acquire. Remind students about rehearsal, etiquette, timelines and safety while conducting surveys. Students should successfully conduct surveys, tabulate and analyze the results. Provide students with an opportunity to assess the effectiveness of their survey.

InfoStar: *Independent*

Teach Through Media Studies

Students are to examine some aspect of the impact newspapers have in their community. They need to design surveys to gather the information they will need for analysis. Provide students with *Design a Survey Rubric* and *Creating a Survey Action Plan* to guide them in the process. Students will individually create a survey and cover letter, carry out the survey research, tabulate the data, and interpret the results.

Gathering the Evidence of Understanding

Conference with the students before they conduct their surveys. Students should be able to create effective surveys, gather their needed data and conduct their research on the impact of newspapers in their community. Have students use the *Design a Survey Rubric, Fig. 15,* to self-evaluate and set goals for next time.

Notes:
Reflect, Rethink, Redesign

◆ How can I scaffold the process of creating effective survey questions?
◆ Are my students aware that when creating their questions it is important to word the question so that it focuses on the required information but that the question does not direct the answer?
◆ How can I best inform students about biased surveys and misuse of data gathering?
◆ Where in local curriculum documents do students have a need for primary data?

Documenting the Evidence

Learner Level
Understanding of Skill
◆ defines the purpose of survey
◆ creates focused questions that target data need
◆ designs an effective, efficient layout for the survey
◆ collects useful data that can be tallied
◆ tallies data accurately
◆ analyzes data

Understanding of Content
◆ values primary data collected
◆ makes connections with curriculum content and real world
◆ uses content vocabulary and terms effectively
◆ interprets the survey data to gain new understanding
◆ uses new learning to predict, solve, decide ...

Design a Survey Rubric (Fig. 8)

Achievement Level	Defines Purpose	Creates Questions	Designs	Collects Data	Analyzes
Level Four	- statements of intent and usage clear, specific, accurate and presented imaginatively - target group clearly identified and realistic in scope - prediction clear and insightful	- range and depth of effective questions insightful - questions effectively address all important areas of the topic - questions are in a logical and well-planned sequence - practiced survey and predicted answers to improve effectiveness of questions	- attractive layout enhanced with relevant graphics - makes effective use of appropriate technologies - alignment of text makes survey completion easy - completion process efficient and self-evident	- all respondents were in the target group - target group breakdown facilitates analysis - all information collected relates directly to the topic - all data collected is easy to tally and chart or graph	- interprets findings and identifies personal/ global consequences - effectively creates and utilizes visual representations to assist with interpretation - makes effective use of appropriate technologies - suggests action/next steps and asks more questions
Level Three	- statement of intent and usage clear, specific and accurate - all appropriate groups targeted - predicts outcome	- clear and concise non-leading questions - enough questions to address all important areas of the topic - questions organized in a logical order - practiced survey and made effective changes where necessary	- layout well organized and easy to read - uses appropriate technologies - answer options are clear - can be completed quickly and easily	- adequate number of target group polled - workable breakdown in range of target group - most data collected relates to the topic and is usable - most data collect can be tallied, charted or graphed	- makes connections and draws logical conclusions - creates visual representations to assist with interpretation - uses appropriate technologies - summarizes findings
Level Two	- statement of intent or usage incomplete, unclear or vague - target group poorly identified - little evidence of an outcome prediction	- questions vague or lead the respondent - questions cover only part of the topic necessary for the survey, too many or too few questions - some indication of planning the order of questions - didn't make necessary adjustments after practice sessions	- layout poorly organized - some evidence of use of use of technologies - answer options are difficult follow - completion is time consuming	- number of people polled inadequate - target group breakdown increments too large or too small - some data unusable - data collected is difficult to tally, chart or graph	- unable to make logical connections - poor or little use of analytical tools - some evidence of use of use of technologies - weak summary
Level One	- statement unclear and vague - target group too broad or too narrow - usage unclear or vague	- questions vague, poorly worded - questions don't "get at" all the needed information - questions in an illogical order - didn't practice survey process before beginning	- no evidence of planning layout, too busy, confusing, no logical order - little or no evidence of use of technology - answer options are difficult to identify - very difficult to complete	- unfinished or inadequate number of surveys - target groups breakdown unrealistic, unworkable - data collected not relevant to topic - data collected cannot be tallied, charted or graphed	- connections are erroneous or non-existant - no evidence of an analytical process - little or no evidence of use of technology - no summary

Interpreting and Evaluating Graphs and Charts
(Fig. 16)

Scan the graph/chart to get a quick overview. If it is effectively designed you should be able to gain all the necessary information quickly. Now read a little closer to interpret the graph/chart and evaluate its effectiveness.

What is the title?

What categories are represented?

What is the date of the study?

Can you tell how the data was collected?

Who produced the graph/chart?

Is there a key or legend? What does it tell you?

What visual techniques have been applied (color, texture, size...)?

What does the graph/chart tell you?

Does it help you to understand the topic better? How?

Is there a better way of representing this information? If so, how, and why?

Is there anything that you can detect that could possibly be misleading? Explain.

On the whole this graph/ chart is (not) effective because.........................

Adapted from *InfoTasks for Successful Learning*, Pembroke Publishers 2001.

Notes:

Creating a Survey Action Plan (Fig.17)

- What is your purpose? What do you think you will discover? Make some predictions.

- What do you plan to do with your results?

- What key data will you focus on in this survey?

- Define your target group(s). Decide how many participants need to complete the survey.

- What format will your survey take? (written, oral, e-mail, web page)

- What types of questions will you develop? (multiple choice, ranking data, short answer, open-ended)

- What prompts do you need to use to gather basic information about the survey participant? (name, age, occupation, etc.)

- Create questions/prompts that will help you gather the data you need. Test these questions with a several people and discuss the effectiveness of each question/prompt.

- Think about what you plan to do with the information and assess the effectiveness and usability of the answers. Will you likely get the kind of information you need?

- Will the information be in a form that allows you to tally, sort etc. and eventually draw conclusions? Redraft your questions, if necessary, and test them again.

- Create a chart/organizer for summarizing your findings and tallying the results.

- Design a neat survey form that includes all the questions you need to ask. Include prompts and/or space to record answers. Time is precious. Keep your survey precise and short so people will to complete it.

- Conduct your survey. Record results accurately. Survey only those in your target group. Thank your participants.

- Tabulate your results and analyze your data. Try creating many different kinds of graphs with your data. Select the graphs that do the best job of visually representing your results. What did you find? How can you use these findings? Can you make connections, draw conclusions, make predictions?

- Compare your results with your predictions. Were there any surprises or disappointments? Would you do anything differently next time?

- Prepare a summary of your survey methods and your results. Who should you share your findings with?

Adapted from Koechlin/Zwaan, *Information Power Pack Intermediate Skillsbook*, Pembroke Publishers 1997.

InfoSkill:

Use Primary Sources
Students will collect and analyze primary sources of information

Skill Discussion

Sometimes the best source of information for a research topic is a primary source. When students are required to conduct an interview or a survey (see pg. 40) they are gathering original primary data.

When students analyze photographs or artifacts from a time period they are also working with first hand information. Primary sources are potentially very engaging for students because they are real, not second hand. Historical primary sources can make the past come alive for students. To optimize these resources students need to learn how to interpret and analyze them. Technology has made it possible to bring many primary artifacts into the classroom virtually.

> **Primary sources** are original records without interpretation.
> Documents, photographs, video footage, art, music, poetry, diaries, interviews, stories, letters, postcards, artifacts, e-mail, raw statistics,
> **Secondary sources** represent a restatement or interpretation of primary information.
> Encyclopedia, newspaper, books, magazines, documentary, Website,
> Note: sometimes information can be both primary and secondary e.g. an old magazine,

Link Up

- Teaching with Primary Sources
  http://www.coshrc.org/arc/education/primsources.htm
- Teaching Canada Resources Primary Documents
  http://www.umaine.edu/canam/k-12outreach/resources/researchresources/primary.htm

- Museums in the USA
  http://www.museumca.org/usa/

- ARC Archival Research Catalog
  http://www.archives.gov/research_room/arc/index.html

Novice: *Collect Artifacts*

Teach through Social Science

In a fashion course, students are to explore the historical evolution of a particular item of apparel (e.g. hats, shoes, blue jeans etc). Set up a whole-class exploratory activity so students will become familiar with a broad range of choices for their personal research. Instruct students to find an item of clothing from their parents and grandparents and older if possible.

Brainstorm with your students ideas for how they can find these items. Discuss the special care of the artifacts and details needed for correct documentation of the items. Provide enough lead-time so students have an opportunity to consult family friends and community groups and gather three or four interesting apparel artifacts. If they cannot find original items, photographs, which are also primary artifacts, can be used.

Gathering Evidence of Understanding

Provide students with a suitable, safe space to set up a temporary museum of their apparel artifacts. Instruct students to sort their items and categorize them. These categories will become the organizational structure of the display. Students should be able to prepare documentation cards to be displayed with each item. They should be able to explain to others how they collected and why they selected each item for the apparel museum.

> Item name:.................................#.............
>
> Approximate time period:................................
>
> Location:..
>
> Loaned by:..

Adaptation

An excursion to a real museum will help students to understand the importance of primary sources. Provide students with clipboards and have them record different types of primary artifacts they discover. Have them make sketches of interesting ways of displaying artifacts. For more ideas visit *Creating a Classroom Museum* at
http://educate.si.edu/resources/lessons/collect/crecla/crecla0a.htm

Apprentice: *Conduct Interviews*

Teach through Social Studies

"What are the roles and responsibilities of community workers in your neighborhood?" is the overall question to guide this student investigation. Read a picture book or watch a video clip to spark the brainstorming of community workers. e.g. nurse, firefighter, bus driver etc. Prepare students for gathering primary data by interview. Together create the interview questions. Discuss safety and etiquette issues. Prepare students with all the equipment they will need for conducting the interview and documenting the data, e.g. permission letter(s), questionnaire, clipboard, tape recorder etc. Give students lots of experience with mock interviews before they actually conduct a real one.

Gathering Evidence of Understanding

Have students work in pairs to conduct the surveys. They should be able to set up a time with the interviewee, conduct the interview and record and share the results of the interviews. See *Tips for Conducting Interviews, Fig. 18.*

InfoStar: *Gather from Virtual Resources*

Teach through History

Students are examining the women's suffrage movement in North America. They will need to collect primary sources of information about the movement and its leaders. Instruct students to start with their school library to get an overview of the era and the important suffragettes. They should locate books containing photographs, speeches, posters, letters, diaries etc. Teach students how to find and use virtual museums on the Internet in search of primary sources to support their investigations. Discuss legal and ethical issues related to copyright of this information. Provide students with analysis tools so they can take notes and document their findings as they explore each primary source. See *Analyzing Primary Sources, Fig. 19.*

Gathering Evidence of Understanding

Students should be able to apply their search strategies to locate primary documents about the women's suffrage movement. They should document their sources on a source sheet and create a hotlist of sites for the virtual documents to provide easy access for analysis and sharing with others during the rest of the study. Students should complete Analizing Primary Sources Fig. 19 for each artifact.

Adaptations

Bookmark primary source sites for younger or less able students or create an online scavenger hunt, hot list or guided tour to scaffold the learning experience.

Notes:
Reflect, Rethink, Redesign

- ◆ How can the library facilitate helping students find artifacts and primary sources?
- ◆ How does the use of primary sources affect student interest in the topic?
- ◆ Where else in the curriculum are students required to use primary sources of information?

Documenting the Evidence

Learner Level
Understanding of Skill
- ◆ differentiates between primary and secondary sources
- ◆ locates artifacts
- ◆ analyzes artifacts to glean information
- ◆ collects information from a variety of primary sources
- ◆ creates effective interview questions
- ◆ conducts interviews effectively and efficiently
- ◆ collects primary data through the interview process
- ◆ records findings in an organized manner
- ◆ collects primary data from virtual sources

Understanding of Curriculum Content
- ◆ acquires firsthand information
- ◆ makes personal connections to the era, event, people...
- ◆ understands the reality of the event, era...

Tips for Conducting Interviews
(Fig. 18)

Planning the Interview
✓ Define the purpose of your interview
  - ✓ What do you know about the topic already?
  - ✓ What do you hope you will find out?
✓ Brainstorm questions you might ask
  - ✓ Think about your purpose.
  - ✓ You may want to ask both fact and opinion questions.
  - ✓ Select 5-6 of your best questions.
  - ✓ Plan the order of your questions.
  - ✓ Conference with your teacher or a learning buddy to test your questions.
  - ✓ Revise questions and prepare a method of recording responses.

Before the Interview
✓ Contact the person to:
  - ✓ Request an interview
  - ✓ Explain your purpose
  - ✓ Set up a time and location
  - ✓ Get permission if you plan to audio tape or videotape
✓ Prepare your questions.
✓ Prepare an organizer for recording your notes.
✓ Practice with a learning buddy.
✓ Revise questions as necessary.

During the Interview
✓ Arrive on time.
✓ Be polite. Don't interrupt.
✓ Listen actively.
✓ Take accurate notes.
✓ Ask the questions you need to have answered.
✓ Ask a few new questions based on what your expert tells you.
✓ Ask if there is something your expert would like to add.
✓ Thank your expert and confirm contact information.

After the Interview
✓ Organize the your information.
✓ Write a summary
  - ✓ Be accurate
  - ✓ Acknowledge direct quotations and paraphrasing of the expert.
✓ Send a thank-you note and a copy of your summary to your expert.
✓ Record your own analysis and reflections of the interview.

How well did you do?

Which questions were most effective? Why?

Next time....

Adapted from *Information Power Pack Intermediate Skillsbook*, Pembroke Publishers 1997.

Analyzing Primary Sources (Fig. 19)

Primary sources hold treasures of information but you may have to dig for them. When you analyze a primary source you are looking for clues to information about a period of time, person, event or issue.

What kind of primary source are you examining?

✓ Artifact	✓ Audio-tape	✓ Music
✓ Letter	✓ Video-tape	✓ Movie
✓ Diary	✓ Interview	✓ Statistics
✓ Map	✓ Newspaper	✓ Report
✓ Advertisement	✓ Magazine	✓ Government record
✓ Certificate	✓ Visual art	✓ Other:

What are you hoping to find out?

Examine the item carefully. Ask yourself lots of questions. Use all your senses. What has attracted your attention? Record what you see, hear, smell, taste or feel that seems really important.

What surprises or puzzles you about this item?

What does it tell you about the individual or group who made/created this item?

How will this item help with your research quest?

What questions do you have about it?

Where might you find answers to your new questions?

Notes:

Part 3: Select, Process, and Record Data

Having located and gathered the best resources for the project, it is time to sort, sift and weigh the data. Students now begin to scrutinize the information much more closely. They need to select the items that exactly meet their information need. This stage of the process requires students to possess a rich repertoire of reading, viewing, and listening skills, some of which are specific to non-fiction texts. It is time to sort facts and opinions and extract specific details. Students learn how to keep a record of needed data using a variety of note-making strategies. They gather citation information and understand how to use their information legally and ethically.

InfoSkill:

Pre-reading Strategies
Students will develop pre-reading strategies for non-fiction.

Skill Discussion

Reading content material is very different from reading a story. Students need practice with a variety of strategies for approaching the reading of non-fiction. These strategies will provide some background knowledge, and help students make connections between what they already know and the new content. Pre-reading strategies also help students predict what the text will be about. To be successful readers of non-fiction text, students must be able to establish a purpose for reading.

All strategies need to be modeled and practiced many times. Copy a section from a non-fiction text and project on a screen. Magazine articles related to the topic, or video clips, can often be used to provide concise examples of text and illustrations when teaching these strategies.

Some Pre-reading Strategies:
brainstorm, discuss topic with a partner, predict, skim, assess prior knowledge, preview headings, question, learn key vocabulary

Link Up

• Reading Quest. Org Making Sense in Social
 Studies: Strategies for Reading Comprehension
 http://curry.edschool.virginia.edu/go/readquest/strat
 /

• Harvey, Stephanie. 1998. *Non-Fiction Matters*.
 New York, Maine: Stenhouse Publishers.

Novice: *Anticipation Guide*

Teach through Environmental Studies

To prepare students for a discussion on the sustainability of Pacific salmon stocks, select several articles on the issues. Include articles written from different perspectives e.g. fishing industry, native peoples, political and environmental groups. Extract five general statements from each article and paraphrase them as succinctly as possible. Record these statements on copies of the organizer *Think, Read, Decide, Fig. 20,* to create an anticipation guide for each article. Give each student a copy of one of the articles, and the accompanying anticipation guide. Instruct students to read the five statements first and react to them, then read the article and state the author's point of view. Finally have students record what they think now. Ask students to pair up with someone else who read the same article and share their ideas.

Gathering Evidence of Understanding

Group students so that each group has representation from all articles reviewed. (Jigsaw technique) Instruct students to use the organizer to report on the author's thinking as well as their own opinions. Groups should be able to record all the issues and brainstorm some possible causes and effects of these issues. Share each group's findings and discuss the effectiveness of the anticipation guide to prepare for reading and for the group analysis and sharing.

Adaptation

Adjust the text to address special needs students, provide a learning buddy or use a videotext instead of a written text.
Students could extend this experience by conducting further research, writing a letter of opinion, making an entry in a learning log, or by demonstrating their new understanding creatively through drama or visual arts.

Apprentice: *Prediction Based on Visual Clues*

Teach though Geography

To begin a study of human population patterns students need to acquire some background knowledge. To prepare them for assigned reading, select and post a few keywords and phrases from the text e.g. settlement, immigration, urbanization, population, distribution, density etc. Invite students to think about connections and make some predictions about the content of the reading.

Review strategies for using visual text clues to skim and scan for an overview of a topic in a non-fiction text.

See *Skim, Scan, Consider, p. 32-33.*

Gathering Evidence of Understanding

Provide students with the organizer *Pre-Reading Quest, Fig. 21.* This activity will help them learn how to make predictions about the content in non-fiction text. Instruct them to skim through the assigned pages paying attention to all the visual clues on the pages. Tell students to use each visual clue to help them guess what the text is about. They need to develop a question for each visual clue. As students are reading they will make point form notes and sketches to answer their own questions.

InfoStar: *Multiple Strategies Independently*

Teach through Science

Students are investigating how and why earthquakes occur as well as how they are measured. They will consult a variety of resources. Review pre-reading strategies and engage students in a discussion about the effectiveness of each strategy for specific kinds of non-fiction text. Chart strategies that can be initiated by students themselves. e.g. brainstorming, predicting, using visual text cues, developing pre-reading questions, discussion with a partner, using sticky notes to record questions and discoveries, using graphic organizers.

Gathering Evidence of Understanding

Observe students as they prepare to read. Look for indications that students are applying pre-reading strategies. Students should be able to explain the pre-reading strategy/strategies they are using and to tell why they selected that strategy.

Notes:
Reflect, Rethink, Redesign

- Do students have sufficient background experience with the general topic?
- Should I read some related nonfiction aloud to familiarize them with the topic and the schema of non-fiction text?
- Are students focused on their purpose for this reading?
- Do they realize that most of the reading they will do in life will be nonfiction?
- Have I provided a variety of non-fiction texts to give students practice approaching them with different strategies?

Documenting the Evidence

Learner Level
Understanding of Skill
- previews headings, subtitles
- skims captions, sidebars
- studies visuals
- checks meaning of bolded text
- recalls prior related knowledge
- questions and predicts content
- exhibits comfort when reading non fiction
- revisits text to locate details

Understanding of Content
- identifies important information in the text
- uses the information gleaned from non fiction text
- forms a point of view about the issue(s)

Teaching Unit Level
- Observe students and note the degree of engagement and focus during these activities.
- Compare student success with and without the focus on pre-reading strategies.
- Share these strategies with other colleagues and discuss results, adaptations, and improvements...

54 - Build Your Own Information Literate School

Think ➡ **Read** ➡ **Decide**

(Fig. 20)

Reading Selection.............................. Name..............................

Statement	Pre-Reading What do you think?		During Reading What does the author say?	Post Reading What do you think now?
1)				
2)				
3)				
4)				
5)				

Pre-Reading Quest (Fig. 21)

Try this strategy to help you learn how to make predictions about the content in non-fiction text. Skim through the pages you are to read. Pay attention to all the visual clues on the pages. Use each visual clue to help you guess what the text is about. Develop a question for each visual clue. As you are reading make point form notes and sketches to answer your own questions.

Text Feature	Your questions	Your quest notes
□ Title □ Subtitles □ Headings		
Pictures and captions		
Other visuals □ Map □ Chart □ Graph □ Cross-section □ Cut away □ Diagram □ Timeline □ Web □ Other □		
Special Text □ Sidebar □ Bolded text □ Colored text □ Italicized text □ Columns □ Framed text □ Other □		

InfoSkill:

Actively Read, View, Listen
Students will actively and productively read, view, and listen to a variety of resources to extract information relevant to their need.

Skill Discussion

Selecting relevant data from text is a very challenging task for students. This process must be modeled many times using a variety of information texts. The information problem or inquiry question should be visibly displayed and constantly referred to. The process of identifying, extracting and recording relevant key points happens almost simultaneously in research. See *Selecting Relevant Data* pg. 62 and *Note-Making Techniques Fig. 29* for strategies to be blended with this skill.

Today's multimedia world provides a bombardment of fast paced, non-linear information bytes. The implications of the new literacies for the 21st century require us to ensure that all students can decode or "read" all formats including non-written texts. We must teach students how to interact with all types of media text. They must be able to actively read, view, listen, hunt for key ideas, develop questions, make connections, and reflect on their discoveries. Students need to be not only active but also critical users of information sources.

Link Up

• 21st Century Literacies
  http://www.kn.pacbell.com/wired/21stcent/index.html

• 21st Century Skills
  http://www.ncrel.org/engauge/skills/indepth.htm

• Media Awareness Network
  http://www.media-awareness.ca

• Sutherland-Smith, Wendy. 2002. *Weaving the Literacy Web: Changes in reading from page to screen.* 662-669) The Reading Teacher Vol. 55, No. 7, 662-669

Novice: *Model and RVL as a Group*

Teach through Social Studies

Students are working collaboratively to explore life in pioneer times. They will specifically compare the lives of children then and now. The focus will be on comparing food, clothing, health, education, recreation, and family life. Immerse students in a rich variety of information sources including stories both print and oral, non-fiction books, videos, pictures, artifacts and speakers. Teach students how to be active users of each kind of information.

Provide charts and cue cards to help students. Model the application of each skill and chart and organize the discovered data together.

Read Non-fiction

• Skim, and scan for an overview.
• Read again for subtopics: titles, subtitles, captions, sidebars, bolded text, tables of contents.
• Read for needed detail: text, photos, illustrations, charts, graphs, maps, cross-sections.

Read Pictures

• What is happening in the picture?
• Which details are important?
• What is new information for me?
• Why is this picture important?

View Video

• Use videotape as you would use print.
• View, view and view again.
• View once for an overview.
• Rewind or fast forward to areas of specific interest. Rewind to view again. Pause to make notes.
• Pay attention to images, words, music, film techniques such as camera angles, use of color...

Listen

• Listen actively and critically.
• Stop all other activities and focus on the audio.
• Look at the speaker.
• Reflect on the message/facts.
• Reflect on the emotions.

Gathering Evidence of Understanding

While students interact with resources to extract the information, question them about which data they are selecting. They should be able to explain why they selected specific data. Students should also be able to articulate the strategies they are using.

Adaptation

Students will need many opportunities to practice active reading, viewing, and listening to information. Provide students with an organizer such as *RVL Connect, Fig. 22,* so they can keep track of their thoughts as they interact with different media texts.

Apprentice: *RVL Online*

Teach through Science

The students are working on an inquiry to determine the impact of the use of an energy source (e.g. fossil fuel) on the hemispheric environment. They have explored the topic, defined and clarified their quest, listed their specific needs on a **KNL** and selected a variety of resources. For this topic students now need to access current periodical databases and Websites. Students need to learn how to make wise choices about which kinds of resources to use to best address their information problem. Guide them to understand the similarities and differences between types of resources. Point out to students that while online information is often more recent they must be more vigilant about its validation.

Instruct students to compare the parts of a non-fiction book to a Website. Have students develop a chart similar to the following.

Non-Fiction Book	Website
Cover	Mainpage/home page
Table of contents	Hypertext links
Author(s)	Author(s)
Publisher	Website owner or sponsor
Copyright date	Copyright date
Headings	Hypertext links
Visuals	Visuals and multimedia images
Contact info	e-mail links
Index	Search tools

Students also need to learn that reading a book is quite different from decoding a Website. The effective and efficient use of online information will require teacher guidance and lots of practice. Teach students some tips for actively using digital

information. Use *Working With Digital Text, Fig. 23, 24,* as a poster or as bookmarks for students.

Gathering Evidence of Understanding

Observe students as they are working and ask them to explain their navigation journey. Students should be able to explain the digital text features they are using with appropriate vocabulary e.g. home page, hypertext links, search box, etc. Students should also be cognizant of when it is best to use print resources and when online resources are better.

InfoStar: *RVL Critically*

Teach through Social Science

Students are preparing to investigate the causes and effects of domestic violence. The sensitive nature of this inquiry requires the validation of resources selected and the critical use of these resources. Students need to be reminded of their active reading, viewing and listening skills. At this point discuss with students some basic concepts of media literacy. Provide contemporary examples the students will be able to identify with, such as ads, TV shows, web sites, and music videos.

Some Key Concepts of Media Literacy
• Media are constructs of reality.
• Media have their own forms, aesthetics, techniques and conventions.
• Media audiences negotiate meaning in texts.
• Media contains beliefs and value messages.
• Media have commercial implications.

Gathering Evidence of Understanding

In small groups have students discuss how media may manipulate information. Have each group develop a list of cautions or "look-fors". e.g. charged words, appeal to emotion, sexual imaging etc. Share and develop a list of tips for critical use of all types of media for research. Students should apply these skills to their work.

Notes: Reflect, Rethink, Redesign
√ Do students require more practice with critical use of digital text?
√ Where else in the curriculum can I infuse meaningful practice with this skill?

Documenting the Evidence

Learner Level
Understanding of Skill
√ uses all kinds of texts effectively
√ applies appropriate search strategies
√ uses special features to navigate
√ interacts with text by questioning
√ checks need and stays on topic

Notes:

RVL Connect (Fig. 22)

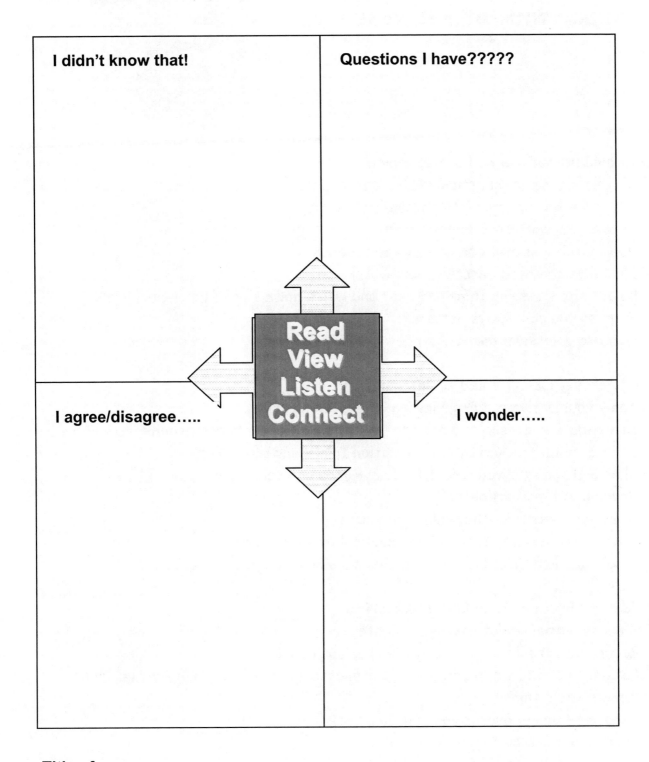

Title of resource...

Kind of resource...

Working With Digital Text
(Fig. 23)

Avoid aimless surfing and site-hopping
- Develop an inquiry question/statement of purpose
- Break down your topic into chunks/sub-topics
- Develop keywords and key phrases
- Use search operators to narrow your search
- Skim hits and read descriptions
- Select the sites you think are best and write down the URLs or bookmark them so you can always get back
- Validate your selected Websites

Avoid getting lost in a sea of information
- Apply your active reading, viewing and listening skills
- Investigate the visuals related to your topic like charts and graphs
- Don't get sidetracked by the animation tricks and glitz.
- Skim and scan for your identified keywords and sub-topics
- Develop web navigation skills
- Use hypertext links that relate to your topic
- When links are "off topic" use the back button to return
- If you get lost, look for a link to the main/home page and start again.

Avoid the threat of accidental plagiarism
- Process gathered data as you navigate
- Record your findings on an organizer as you go along
- Cut and paste to a notepad or word processing file information that requires more critical thinking
- Record all direct quotes you plan to use and proper citations
- Record all referencing information
- Bookmark the site so you can easily return to it

Working With Digital Text

Avoid the threat of accidental plagiarism

✓ Process gathered data as you navigate

✓ Record your findings on an organizer as you go along

✓ Cut and paste to a notepad or word processing file information that requires more critical thinking

✓ Record all direct quotes you plan to use and proper citations

✓ Record all referencing information

✓ Bookmark the site so you can easily return to it

Working With Digital Text

Avoid the threat of accidental plagiarism

✓ Process gathered data as you navigate

✓ Record your findings on an organizer as you go along

✓ Cut and paste to a notepad or word processing file information that requires more critical thinking

✓ Record all direct quotes you plan to use and proper citations

✓ Record all referencing information

✓ Bookmark the site so you can easily return to it

Working With Digital Text

Avoid the threat of accidental plagiarism

✓ Process gathered data as you navigate

✓ Record your findings on an organizer as you go along

✓ Cut and paste to a notepad or word processing file information that requires more critical thinking

✓ Record all direct quotes you plan to use and proper citations

✓ Record all referencing information

✓ Bookmark the site so you can easily return to it

Fig. 24

InfoSkill:

Select Relevant Data

Students will identify and select relevant data from a variety of non-fiction resources and record the key points.

Skill Discussion

Extracting relevant data from someone else's words is a difficult skill to teach and a difficult concept for young researchers to grasp. At this stage of the process students are examining secondary sources and applying their active reading, viewing and listening skills to hunt for those nuggets of information that will help them with their quest. They need to explore the ideas of others before they can start to build their own understanding. Extracting the relevant data, recording it accurately and keeping it in a safe place until they are ready to process it is the aim of this exercise. Relevance, accuracy, precision and academic honesty are key elements.

Think About It, Fig. 25

Think About It!

Use these prompts to help you process the sources you have gathered:

• What do you need to find out?

• Can you use this source?

• Is this what you are looking for?

• Identify and select the important points.

• Stop and check your progress

Link Up

• Koechlin, C. and Zwaan, S. 2001. *Info Tasks for Successful Learning: Building Skills in Reading, Writing, and Research.* Markham, ON: Pembroke.

Novice: *Model Identifying and Selecting*

Teach through Science

Students are investigating animal habitats and looking for similarities and differences. With the class, decide on the elements to be compared e.g. animal life, plant life, natural environment, stability etc. Model the extrac-ting and recording process. Prepare a large chart with the elements as headings. Share a variety of resources on a specific habitat e.g. non-fiction book, video, Internet site. Demonstrate a number of strategies for identifying the relevant key points for this inquiry. Model using "think aloud" prompts to help students understand that they need to be actively thinking as they work.

When students are ready to work independently provide them with a copy of *Think About It, Fig. 25,* and instruct them to keep referring to it as they gather their data.

Some strategies to share:

• Review active reading, viewing and listening skills by demonstration.

• Use sticky notes to mark places to return to and to record reflections in print resources.

• Chunk video viewing. Stop and discuss relevant discoveries and record key data. Continue viewing

• Copy and paste a relevant section of a website or online article to word processing. Print and use a highlighter to identify needed data

• Provide lots of strategies for recording point form notes. See *Note-Making Techniques Fig. 29.*

Gathering Evidence of Understanding

Observe students as they work independently to find relevant data for their assigned habitat. Students should be using *Think About It* prompts to help them zero in on the precise data they need. Students should be able to select key points and record them accurately.

Adaptation

Pre-readers can still be engaged in inquiry through lots of discussion and teacher recording of ideas. Use non-fiction Big Books to learn about discovery of information with very young students. Teach students how to find information in pictures and other visuals. Invite students to record their discoveries in drawings. As literacy skills develop use reflective prompts to guide recording e.g. I discovered..., I know that....., I think that.......

Apprentice: *Examine for Inconsistencies*

Teach through Geography

Students are gathering statistical data about their country. They will enter this information in a database and continue to gather data about several countries in each continent. Students will use the database to develop and analyze graphs to discover global relationships and patterns. As a class, decide on the specific statistics to be collected and then determine fields for the database, e.g. population, area of country, main industries etc. Group the students in triads. Instruct each triad to find 3 different sources of statistical data about the country they are working on. Each student will fill out a chart recording the needed data using one of the sources they located. Ask students to examine the data to discover and note discrepancies or inconsistencies. Debrief with students and discuss what can be done to determine which information is correct.

Gathering Evidence of Understanding

Discuss the implication of this exercise with regard to searches for information in the future and interpretation of printed statistics. Students should be able to explain how they checked for authority, currency and intent of statistical data in order to select what was appropriate

InfoStar: *Analyze for Quantity and Quality*

Teach through Global Issues

Students are engaged in independent studies. They are at the stage of embarking on analysis of their data. Before proceeding they need to stop and think about the quantity and quality of the information they have gathered. Each student should use this check list to assess the information gathered to date then revisit the locating stage of the process to find any other additional resources and data to complete their notes.

Data Check Point (See also Fig. 24a)

- Do you have enough data to address your inquiry question?
- Is all the data on topic?
- Are you excited about what you have discovered?
- What perspectives have been included?

- Whose voice is missing?
- Do you have any conflicting data?
- Do you see any trends or patterns?
- What have you learned?
- What do you still need to find out?
- Where will you look next for needed data?
- Have you kept track of sources of quotes and paraphrased ideas?

Gathering Evidence of Understanding

Instruct students to make an appointment with a peer and to share working notes. Invite students to critique one another's work, looking for gaps and checking relevance and adequacy. Students should use *Data Check Point, Fig. 24a*, to assess partners' notes. Individually students develop a plan to again go back and revisit necessary stages in the process to address concerns and fill in the gaps in their collected information if needed.

Notes: Reflect, Rethink, Redesign

Do students understand how mastering this skill will make their data management more efficient and their assignments more successful?

Documenting the Evidence

Learner Level

Understanding of Skill

√ applies suggested strategies to identify relevant data

√ develops and adopts personal strategies

√ applies suggested strategies for note-making

√ follows questions and prompts in *Think About It*:
- to evaluate the sources and resources
- to identify and select data
- to check and evaluate progress

√ uses the questions in *Data Check Point* to analyze data for quality and completeness

Understanding Curriculum Content

√ identifies and uses relevant and accurate information

√ topic-related assignments are more precise, concise, and focused

√ improvement in quality and quantity of information used

√ improved scope of perspectives

√ improved clarity in understanding of key concepts

√ more accurate decisions, conclusions

√ more plausible opinions

Data Check Point (Fig.24a)

Use the check points on this chart to help you assess the quantity and quality of the data you have gathered so far. Use the notes column to keep track of your plans for improvement.

Check Points	Notes
• Do you have enough data to address your inquiry question?	
• Is all the data on topic?	
• Are you excited about what you have discovered?	
• Do you have any conflicting data?	
• Do you see any trends or patterns?	
• Have you kept track of sources of quotes and paraphrased ideas	
What perspectives have been included?	
Whose voice is missing?	
What have you learned?	
What do you still need to find out?	
Where will you look next for needed data?	
Next Steps...	

Think About It! (Fig. 25)

Use these prompts to help you process the sources you have gathered.

What do you need to find out?

- Actively read, view, and listen.

- Skim and scan for keywords and phrases

- Watch for specific information.

Can you use this source?

- Which data answers your question, problem, or focus?

- What is interesting but not needed for this task?

Is this what you are looking for?

- What is repetitive?

Identify and **select** important points.

- Note what you need. Use stickies.

- Use an organizer to take notes.

- Make mental pictures.

- Make point form note.

- Make sketches.

- Is the information factual?

- How can you verify it?

Stop and **check** your progress.

- Have you found interesting information?

- Do you have enough information?

- Where are the gaps?

- Talk to a friend or teacher about what you have

  recorded.

- Are some perspectives, conditions, aspects... missing?

- Where can you find out more?

InfoSkill:

Determine Fact
Students will compare information sources to determine what is fact.

Skill Discussion

As students work with a variety of resources, they are often frustrated or confused by the conflicting information they detect. They need practice discovering and confirming factual information. Young students learn to sort fact from fiction and progress to sorting facts from opinions and ultimately making personal links or reactions to the information they select.

I Wonder Chart

Wonder	Fiction	Non-fiction book	Non-fiction video
What do they eat?	bears eat honey	bears eat honey	they eat fish, and berries
Do they have a home?	they have a house	bears live in the woods	mother makes a den
What do they do all day?			
How do they look after their babies?			

Link Up

- Education World: Fact Fiction or Opinion Evaluating Online Information
  http://www.education-world.com/a_curr/curr194.shtml

- Strategies for Empowering Students: Is it what I think or what I know?
  http://www.urbanext.uiuc.edu/ce/strat123.html

Novice: *Fact and Fiction*

Teach Through Science

Students will explore the basic needs of some animals they are familiar with. First discuss with students some of the basic things children need to stay healthy and happy. Then, work with students to develop a list of "*I wonder...*" questions that they will use to explore and discover the basic needs of an animal. Show a popular children's video or read a fictional story about a familiar animal such as *Winnie the Pooh*. Chart the answers to the "I wonder..." questions based on the fiction story/video. See the *I Wonder Chart*. Then read from a non-fiction book and chart the answers to I wonder questions. Show a short non-fiction video about the same animal and again ask the questions and record the new answers in the appropriate column. Your chart should look something like the *I Wonder Chart* at the side. Show the students a picture of a teddy bear and a picture of a real brown bear. Talk about real and imaginary to lead into an explanation of the meaning of fiction and fact. Help students to understand that information in the stories is often imaginary although the authors use some facts to build their stories, while the information in non-fiction books and non-fiction videos tells facts about real bears. Review the chart and highlight factual information.

Gathering Evidence of Understanding

Have students make a fact booklet about brown bears. Students should be able to record an "I wonder ..." question and a factual answer on each page. Instruct students to illustrate each page. Remind students to make pictures of real brown bears. The colors they are using and the environment they are drawing the bear in should reflect what they have discovered to be fact. Have students share their fact booklets with each other.

Adaptation

Follow up with other storybook animals and create fact (real) and fiction (imaginary) books, charts, bulletin boards, displays, mural, etc. Develop book bags to go home that contain a fact book and a fiction book about an animal. Write up an explanation page for parents so they can follow up on reinforcing this skill.

Apprentice: *Fact and Opinion*

Teaching Through Science

Students are working on a research project involving an environmental issue such as smog, clear cutting, or use of fossil fuels to produce energy. The information sources on these topics may contain bias. Students must analyze to determine what is actual fact and what is the opinion of the author. Discuss and list characteristics of fact and opinion and trigger words that often accompany opinions. Identify ways of confirming what is deemed to be factual.

Facts
- events that actually occurred
- information that is exact and provable
- information that is specific and accurate
- dates, names, quantities

Opinions
- views, thoughts, feelings and judgments
- conclusions that cannot be proved
- words and phrases such as virtually, clearly, no doubt, most, almost none, it is apparent, etc.

Model the process of determining facts and opinions. Select an article and prepare it for projection on a screen. Use different colored highlighters to indicate facts and opinions as the students discover them.

Gathering Evidence of Understanding

Instruct students to make point form notes from the articles and texts that they have gathered. Have the students review their point form notes and indicate with colored highlighters facts and opinions.

InfoStar: *React to Facts and Opinions*

Teaching Through World Issues

Once students are skilled at determining fact from opinion, raise the level of this analysis skill by inviting students to react to and discuss the information. For an exploratory activity in preparation for a world issues topic such as famine or children's' rights, gather a variety of resources, both print and non-print, on the topic. Pair students and provide each pair with an item related to the topic. Allow students adequate time to read, view, and or listen to the item. Instruct student A to record facts from the resource and beside each fact to record a question related to the fact. Have student B record opinions from the same resource and beside each opinion record a

personal reflection related to the opinion. After ten minutes or so ask students to switch roles. Allow at least fifteen minutes for students to share their questions and reflections and to discuss their findings.

Gathering Evidence of Understanding

Have students individually select another resource and complete the organizer *Linking to Facts and Opinions, Fig. 26.* Instruct students to write an entry in their learning log recording their reactions to this strategy. Students should identify any problems they had distinguishing between fact and opinion and articulate how they made their final decisions. They should also explain how the role reversals and discussions enhanced their understanding of the topic and clarified their thoughts about what was fact and what was opinion.

Notes:
Reflect, Rethink, Redesign

√ Can students make connections to see the need for applying this skill in other areas of the curriculum?
√ How can I help students see the real life applications for this skill?

Documenting the Evidence

Learner Level
Understanding of Skill
√ identifies fiction
√ determines fact
√ differentiates between fact and fiction
√ notices opinion presented as fact
√ identifies opinion
√ differentiates between fact and opinion
√ checks for proof of "facts"
√ considers the possible reasons for presenting opinion as fact

Understanding Curriculum Content
√ collects less but more accurate data
√ uses validated facts
√ makes decisions, forms opinions and conclusions based on factual information
√ makes more accurate decisions, opinions and conclusions

Notes:

Linking to Facts and Opinions (Fig. 26)

Name: ....

Topic: ....

Facts	My Questions	Opinions	My Reactions

Perhaps...

Adapted from InfoTasks for Successful Learning, Pembroke Publishers 2001

InfoSkill:

Read Pictures
Students will decode information from video, pictures in books, and photographs in newspapers and magazines, to discover implicit and explicit information messages they contain.

Skill Discussion

Illustrations and photographs in both fiction and non-fiction texts hold a wealth of information. While some information is very obvious, much of the information must be uncovered. Students need experiences decoding this kind of visual information, as well as opportunities to analyze it. This skill will prepare students for broader visual literacy skills. These skills are critical to information processing today since so much of the information students access is loaded with powerful images. Critical reading of visual images is necessary to uncover all the intended information. Reading pictures will help students to analyze:
• picture books
• non-fiction illustrations
• photographs
• newspaper and magazine photos
• posters
• billboards
• advertisements
• video images
• internet visuals
• virtual museum items

Link Up

• Moline, Steve. 1995. *I See What You Mean: • Children at Work with Visual Information K-8.* Portland ME: Stenhouse.

• Reading Pictures http://www.learn.co.uk/ default.asp?WCI=Unit&WCU=397

• International Visual Literacy Association http://www.ivla.org/

• Visual Literacy http://www.fno.org/PL/vislit.htm

• American Memory - Constructing the Context http://memory.loc.gov/ammem/ndlpedu/lessons/99/ road/fourth.html

Novice: *Guided Response to Prompts*

Teach Through Social Studies

Reading Pictures is an engaging strategy for introducing a social studies topic. The strategy allows students to gain an overview of the new topic while they also make connections to what they already know.

Model this process with the class using an informative poster, a transparency on an overhead, or screen capture from the Internet. Select an illustration or photograph that will provide information related to any social studies topic you are studying e.g. Ancient China, rural communities, or Arctic explorers. Ask students for first reactions to the illustration/photograph. Then continue to scaffold student thinking with prompts:

• Where is this scene located?
• What time period is this?
• What is happening in the picture?
• What might have happened just prior to the picture?
• What might happen next?
• Who do you see in the picture?
• Who do you not see that might be involved? Why?
• What might have happened after the picture?

Model the process with several pictures dealing with aspects of the social studies topic you want students to start thinking about e.g. Rural communities - wheat farm, ski lodge, fishing community, apple orchard, cattle ranch cottage, etc.

Gathering Evidence of Understanding

Instruct students to find a picture about the topic being studied. Students should be able to apply the picture reading skill to this picture. They should read the picture and respond to each prompt. Have students form small groups and share their picture responses. Debrief with the entire class and look for common understandings as well as creative thought.

Adaptation

This strategy works well for short video clips on a topic as well. Teach students how to view once, rewind and view again for specific detail. Picture reading prepares students for writing about a topic. Adapt the prompts to guide the thinking and writing process.

Apprentice: *Develop Simple Questions*

Teach Through Language Arts

Model the process with a picture from a big book. Invite students to "read the picture with their eyes". Guide the students' observation with a series of questions beginning with the 5Ws and "How". Print the question starter words on large cards and show the appropriate card for each question.

Who is riding a bike?
What is under the tree?
Where is the mouse hiding?
When will the child wake up?
Why is the kite in the tree?
How will the goat get across the river?

Ask a few students to think up questions to ask about the picture and display the correct question starter card as they ask the question. Discuss student responses to the questions.
Then read the story and enjoy.

Gathering Evidence of Understanding

Pair students up and give each group a set of question starter words. Ask students to select an illustrated book they would like to "picture read" together. They should be able to create questions using the question starters. Give each pair of students a chart and ask them to record with a checkmark each time they use a starter question word. Students will use all the question starters at least once. Students will take turns asking and responding to each other's questions about the pictures.

Provide a chart to record student use of question starters so students can self assess their use of variety in question types.

Who	What	When	Where	Why	How
√	√	√	√	√	√
√			√	√	
√					

Adaptation

Learning how to read pictures enables and enhances information access for all learners, especially for non-readers and second language learners. Care is needed when selecting pictures for information access. Just as with text, look for authority and accuracy of the visual information.

InfoStar: *Question and Look for Relationships*

Teach Through Visual Arts

Model this process with students using a photograph from a current newspaper or magazine of interest to your students.

Ask students to brainstorm questions about the picture. Chart questions. When you have 10 or 12 questions stop and cut up the chart so each question is on a separate piece of paper. Ask students to look for connections in the questions, then together sort and cluster questions. Arrange them around the picture in a web to create an artistic piece.

Have students respond to questions and give explanations for their responses.

Gathering Evidence of Understanding

Each student finds a photograph from a newspaper or magazine and generates 10-20 questions about the photograph. They should analyze what they see by first sorting and clustering the questions into categories, then answering the questions. Students will display their critical reading of the photo by creating a creative question and answer collage web.

Notes: Rework, Rethink, Redesign
√ How can I ensure that students are creating questions that guide their analysis to the background as well as the foreground?
√ How could I utilize this skill in the exploration stage of a new research topic?

Documenting the Evidence
Learner Level

Understanding of Skill
√ appreciates pictures as a valuable source of information
√ uses prompts to analyze pictures
√ creates questions to systematically
√ analyze the information contained in pictures
√ applies picture-reading strategies to interpret and analyze a variety of illustrative materials
√ considers and validates intent, accuracy and authority of pictures

Understanding of Content
√ gleans lots of information quickly
√ not handicapped by poor reading skills
√ improved interest in topic
√ greater attention to detail

InfoSkill:

Use Features of Non-Fiction Text
Students will use the features of non-fiction text to determine usefulness and to extract needed information.

Skill Discussion

The decoding of expository text requires a different set of skills from reading narrative. Non-fiction texts consist of a combination of various forms of information writing and visual texts. Providing many opportunities to read, view and listen to non-fiction text will help students to become familiarized with the range of texts available. Teaching students how to best use non-fiction texts requires providing practice deconstructing as well as constructing it. If students are to be successful researchers it is imperative that they learn how to make use of the features of non-fiction text that can help them readily access needed information.

Non-fiction text must be recognized as legitimate literature. (Jobe 2002) Many students prefer non-fiction to fiction and there are sound pedagogical reasons for supporting and enhancing their interest in non-fiction.

Link Up

- InfoActive.
  http://www.longman.com.au/infoactive/home.html

- International Reading Association: Exploring How Section Headings Support Understanding of Expository Texts.
  http://www.readwritethink.org/lessons/lesson_view.asp?id=24

- International Visual Literacy Association
  http://www.ivla.org/index.htm

- Harvey, Stephanie. 1998. *Non-fiction Matters*. York Maine: Stenhouse.

- Jobe, Ron and Mary Dayton-Sakari. 2002. *Info-Kids*. Markham ON: Pembroke Publishers.

- Moline, Steve. 2001. *Show Me! : teaching information and visual texts 1-2, 3-4, 5-6* Richmond Hill ON: Scholastic Canada Ltd.

- Beers,Karlene. "NoTime, No Interest, No Way" Pt.2 (1996). *School Library Journal*.

Novice: *Model Use of Features of Text*

Teach through Science

In preparation for a unit of study on the structure and function of vital organs in the human body, collect informative visual texts e.g. charts, big books, transparencies, visuals from non-fiction books, projections of Internet visuals. Find examples of cross-sections, cutaways, tables, graphs, flowcharts etc. Share these samples with students and work with them to extract the information about a specific body organ. Chart the information discovered.

Gathering Evidence of Understanding

Assign small groups of students to select a body organ and find visual texts about it. Instruct the students to read those visuals, extract information, and write a brief report on the structure and function of the organ. Students should be able to glean information from the visuals and accurately rework that information into a report.

Adaptations

Conversely when students are familiar with the range of visual texts used in non-fiction materials they need opportunities to turn information text into a visual text. Teach students how to create visual information using word processing and draw tools. Provide students with instruction in using and creating:
- timelines
- storyboards
- webs
- flow charts
- tables
- cross section diagrams
- cut away diagrams
- maps
- graphs
- sketches

Apprentice: *Use a Range of Features of Text*

Teach through Social Studies

Groups of students are preparing to investigate ancient civilizations. Model how to make use of specific features of non-fiction text so students can work more efficiently and effectively to locate needed information. Use a few selected pages from a very visual text to teach the skill (photocopy or project). Using both teacher think aloud questioning and student responses, walk through the pages with students. Explain how each feature can help researchers to locate needed information.

Record findings on a chart such as *Using Visual Clues* (see also Fig. 27).

Using Visual Clues

Text Feature	What do you see?	Why is it important?
Title		
Subtitles		
Headings		
Pictures		
Captions		
Visuals: map, chart, graph, diagram, timeline...		
Sidebars		
Bolded/Colored Text		
Glossary		
Text Blocks /Framed Text		

Gathering Evidence of Understanding

Have students find a non-fiction text on their topic. Instruct students to practice their new skill of using features of non-fiction text by completing the organizer *Using Visual Clues, Fig. 27).* Students should be able to find samples of each feature and record what they see and what they have learned about their topic from that feature.

InfoStar: *Apply Features of Text*

Teach through Technology

Provide students with a simple device e.g. stapler, hole punch, egg timer etc. Instruct students to write a procedure manual for using the simple machine. Students must apply their knowledge of procedure writing and use suitable features of text to help the reader access and understand the information needed to operate the machine.

Gathering Evidence of Understanding

Students develop a checklist to self-evaluate their manual. Students should assess their ability to use features of text to communicate information. Organize students in pairs. Have them follow their partner's procedures to use the simple machine and apply their checklists to evaluate the procedures.

Notes:
Reflect, Rethink, Redesign

√ Do my students understand how this strategy will help them to select and gather data more efficiently?

√ Do students now have more time to focus on higher level activities in the research quest?

√ Do students realize that they can now identify the main idea of the material more quickly?

√ Which students benefited most from these strategies? Why?

Documenting the Evidence

Teaching Unit Level

√ Compare the amounts of time students spent identifying and extracting information, before lessons and practice with these strategies, to the amount spent after.

√ Look at not only the time they required but also note the frustration levels and the quantity and relevance of data collected.

√ Record evidence of improvement in the quality of data students acquired.

√ Note the effect on student interest in the task.

Learner Level
Knowledge of Curriculum Content
√ predicts main idea of text
√ makes connections during reading
√ gleans information without having to struggle with difficult vocabulary
√ gleans information from previously inaccessible sources
√ maintains interest in topic

Notes:

Using Visual Clues (Fig. 27)

Searching for the right information can be time consuming.
Use this organizer to help you skim and scan for clues.

Topic/Focus question:…………………………………………………………………………………………..……………

Keywords and phrases: …….

Text Feature	What do you see?	What can you learn?
Title		
Subtitles		
Headings		
Pictures and captions		
Visuals	▪ Map ▪ Chart ▪ Graph ▪ Cross-section ▪ Cut away ▪ Diagram ▪ Timeline ▪ Web ▪ Other ▪	
Text blocks / Framed text	▪ Sidebars ▪ Bolded text ▪ Colored text ▪ Italicized text ▪ Framed text ▪ Columns ▪ Other ▪	

InfoSkill:
Note-making
Students will develop note-making skills and a variety of strategies for organizing the selected data.

Skill Discussion

Once students have identified and gathered the best sources of information for their inquiry they must prepare to collect the data they need to answer their inquiry question. Students now need to be taught how to identify the information they need and develop a variety of strategies for keeping all this information organized. When students are taking notes from their sources they are already starting to analyze their data. By putting this data in their own words or reinterpreting it in another form they are demonstrating their understanding of key concepts and the ideas of others. Encourage students to also record their own ideas and connections.

Research notes must be:
- **Accurate** - Be very careful to record correct information
- **Honest** - Always credit words and ideas of others
- **Concise** - Be brief, use abbreviations, keywords and phrases
- **Organized** - Always use a technique to keep your notes organized
- **Relevant** - keep checking your data. Does it help to answer your question? Are you staying on topic?

Link Up

- Quoting, Paraphrasing and Summarizing
  http://owl.english.purdue.edu/handouts/research/r_quotprsum.html
- Note-Making; Note Layout
  http://learnline.ntu.edu.au/studyskills/nm/nm_nl.html
- Study Skills Guide to Note-Making
  http://www.leeds.ac.uk/ics/study2.htm

Novice: *Sketches and Jottings*

Teach through Science

When students are developmentally ready, teach them how to make sketches and diagrams to display their understanding of the world of nature e.g. sketch of a tree, an ant farm, cross section of a fruit etc. Conference with each student and assist them to label their drawings with words and arrows.

When reading and comprehension levels are appropriate introduce the strategy of recording key ideas in jottings.

Begin by modeling, first follow *Tips for Jot Notes*, then have students explore non-fiction texts to uncover specific information and record key data e.g. discover the uses of soil.

Tips for Jot Notes
- Read, view, listen for an overview
- Re-read, view, listen for important ideas
- Record only key ideas
- Begin each jot note with a nugget
- No sentences
- No need for punctuation
- Use abbreviations and numbers
- Be brief
- Do not record anything you do not understand

Gathering Evidence of Understanding

Students should be able to record information in labeled sketches and jottings and explain their meaning. Hold a peer/teacher conference with each student and ask them to tell the story of their research and explain the discoveries they have recorded.

Adaptations

Model sketching, making diagrams, labeling and making jot notes. Use a projector and highlighters or photocopy information so you can highlight key phrases and ideas.

Provide students with ready-made organizers at first so they can keep their data organized. To limit the space for writing and aid the jotting process, try folding paper into columns or give students sticky notes or index cards for recording.
Caution: Even when modeling and teaching, always have a purpose for the skill of note-making. Provide an inquiry question, or series of questions, to frame the need for the information. Link it to the curriculum being studied.

Apprentice: *Variety of Techniques*

Teach through History

Students are engaged in a study of the impact of World War I and they have been asked to discover how events related to this war impacted on their local community. The nature of this assignment will necessitate that students not only gather data, but also process that data to build an understanding of the impact. Students will need many strategies to help them gather and record the data they acquire from both primary and secondary sources. Introduce Note-Making Fig. 29.

Remind students of note-making techniques and encourage them to try a variety.

• Highlighting
• Sticky notes
• Split page notes
• Index cards
• 5R Method
• SQ4R Method
• Graphic organizers
• Visual representation

See *Note-Making Techniques, Fig. 29,* for details.

Gathering Evidence of Understanding

Have students try out a few different techniques for taking notes. Assess the notes as a valued component of the project. (See Fig. 28 Note-Making Rubric).

InfoStar: *Electronic Notes*

Teach through Literature

Students are to select two novels having a common theme and compare and evaluate the character development. Students will need to consult the work of professional critics. Many of their sources will be online. Often the time in the lab is limited so students must know how to make use of special features of online resources. Some Web Sites and databases allow saving to a disc or e-mailing so the article can be reviewed later. If students are making notes as they search it is often expedient to open a word processing document and cut and paste pertinent data and quotes into the document to be worked with later. Remind students to also keep careful documentation of each source they have actually used so they have all the information they need for citations.

Once students have retrieved all the relevant data needed, they proceed with processing and making point form notes, as they would from any print resource. Review the basic guidelines and purposes for note-making.

When you are making notes you will generally be making one of three kinds:

Summarizing

When you summarize you condense ideas, details, and supporting arguments in point form using your own words. Summarizing is useful for recording facts, statistics, and background material.

Paraphrasing

When you paraphrase, you take an author's idea, select what is pertinent, and restate it in your own words using your own sentence structure. Make sure you keep the author's meaning.

Direct Quotations

When you use direct quotations you copy the material directly from your source because it is important to use the author's words exactly. Make sure you copy the material carefully and record a reference so you can find it again and cite the source.

Adapted from *Student Research Guide*, 2002, Toronto District School Board

Gathering Evidence of Understanding

Students should apply note-making techniques that work well for them. They should have high standards for the quality of their notes and always maintain academic honesty.

Notes:
Reflect, Rethink, Redesign
√ Do students understand the purpose of their note-making?
√ How can the entire department, school ensure that note-making is valued?
√ What is the connection between effective note-making and academic honesty?

Documenting the Evidence

Learner Level
Understanding the Skill
√ selects relevant data
√ records accurately and concisely
√ records only useful data
√ organizes notes
√ credits words and ideas of others
√ uses appropriate note taking methods

Notes:

Note Making Rubric (Fig. 28)

Achievement Level	Identifies Information Need	Identifies Data	Gathers	Organizes
Level Four	- has a clear vision of information need - articulates a manageable research question/problem and plans for note making - clearly explains and understands purpose for note making - predicts findings and explains how data will be used	- skims and scans text to identify data relevant to need - reads, views, listens critically, to select pertinent supporting details - reflects, sifts, and evaluates quality and quantity of data - utilizes all the features of non-fiction text	- records all relevant data - all data is on topic and necessary to fulfill need - includes enriching data that enhances focus - makes connections to prior knowledge - reworks data into another format to build understanding - adds personal reflections and questions	- creates and utilizes recording organizers that are specific to information need - develops a personal note making technique - records all citation and reference information using an organizer
Level Three	- understands information need - articulates a manageable research question/problem - identifies purpose of note taking - plans use of data	- skims and scan text to identify main points - reads, views and listens to select supporting details - evaluates quantity and quality of data - uses most features of non-fiction text	- includes main ideas - all data is on topic - all data supports the focus - amount of data is adequate to meet need - includes personal reactions to gathered data	- selects and uses data organizers appropriate to information need - selects and applies appropriate note making strategies - records all necessary citation and reference information
Level Two	- some confusion about information need - research question requires some clarification - purpose for note making requires some clarification - incomplete plan for data use (fails to connect research question/problem with note making)	- has some knowledge of strategies required to skim, scan - reads, views, listens but has difficulty identifying needed data - checks for quantity of data - works with a limited number of non-fiction text features	- includes some main ideas - data is on topic but not all relevant to need - too much data or inadequate data - little evidence of personal responses	- selects inappropriate strategies or organizers - applies simple note taking strategies - records some referencing information
Level One	- doesn't understand information need - research question unclear - no focus for note making - no plan for using data	- demonstrates little ability to skim and scan - has difficulty concentrating on text - fails to evaluate data gathered - doesn't benefit from features of non fiction text	- missing most main ideas - data doesn't fulfill information need - much of data gathered is extraneous or irrelevant - no reflection or reaction evident	- doesn't use an organizer - records data randomly - little evidence of reference records

Note-Making Techniques (Fig. 29)

You have **identified and gathered** the best sources of information for your inquiry. Now you need to **make notes** of the data you need to answer your inquiry question. Your teacher will assess these notes. They are a vital part of research. As you take notes from your sources you are starting to **analyze** your data. Putting this data in your own words **demonstrates your understanding** of key concepts and the ideas of others. Remember to also **record your own ideas thoughts and questions** as they come to you. You will need to use these reflections when you are ready to write your thesis or prepare for a presentation.

If you use one of these note-making techniques or a combination of them you will not be plagiarizing.

Note-Making Organizers	• Use teacher-made organizers or make your own. • Use sub-headings to separate information. • Use arrows, shapes and colors to help you organize data and identify relationships. • Summarize or paraphrase the information in point form, using your own words. • Be sure to include page numbers, and put quotation marks around direct quotations.
Index Cards	• Use a separate index card for each source or use an index card for each sub-topic. • Write a question on each card then record appropriate notes. • Record notes on one side of the card only so you can spread them out and sort and organize them later. • Keep a numbered source sheet of all resources used. • Use numbers to identify sources on your index cards. • As you work, follow tips for note-making.
5 R Method	• Fold a page in four columns. Label the top of columns using - **record, relate, reduce** and **reflect.** • As you read each book or article, make point form notes of the important ideas and write them in the **"record"** column. • Put quotation marks around direct quotes and record page numbers. • In the **"relate"** column jot down any connected ideas or information you already know about this topic. • Think about your own personal knowledge, media, books and people who relate to this topic. • When you have finished making notes, reduce the information to three to five main ideas and write them in the **"reduce"** column. These ideas may eventually become the paragraph or section headings of your essay/presentation. • Finally think about the theme of this book/article and write it down in your own words in the **"reflect'** column. Add your own ideas about why this is important. This may become the main thesis of your final product or one of the main arguments to support your thesis.
Split Page Notes	• Fold your paper in half. Try one of these methods of note-making. • On one side record headings and sub headings. On the other side record factual data and ideas, quotations related the heading. • **Or** on one side record point form notes and on the other side record your personal reflections or questions you have about that information. • **Or** on one side record point form notes and on the other side try to make that information visual. Create a web, chart, sketch or graph that will help you to analyze that information.

Sticky Notes	• Skim through books/articles and use sticky notes to mark sections you want to go back to when you are ready to make formal notes. • Record keywords, phrases or questions you have. Capture this spontaneous thinking is important. • Use sticky markers to help you to quickly make citations when you are ready to prepare your product or presentation.
Highlighting	• Only use this technique only on photocopied material or on your own notes. • Skim through the photocopy to highlight keywords and ideas. Avoid highlighting too much. • Use different colored highlighters for different sub-topics or relationships. Read carefully and make point form notes. • Use highlighters to help you reduce your own point form notes or to cluster ideas in preparation for writing your essay/presentation.
Visual	• Create webs or map ideas. • Very effective for note-making while viewing a video. • It is also a great technique to use to pull all your notes together and start to analyze them. It will help you sort out your notes and look for connected and conflicting ideas.
SQ4R Method	• Define your need. What is your purpose for studying, reading, and researching this material? • **S**urvey or skim the work quickly. • **Q**uestion. List several questions you have about the text. • **R**ead the material to find the answers to your questions. • **R**ecite what you have discovered to yourself or a buddy. • **R**ecord main ideas. • **R**eview. Did I find out what I needed? What questions do I still have?
Word Processing	• All of the above note-making techniques can be word-processed. • Word processing tools can save you time and allow you to quickly rearrange or edit your information e.g. changes to font, highlighting, editing features and spellchecker. • Caution: Check with your teachers. They may want you to print your work in progress at regular intervals so they can assess your progress during conferences. • Remember to save your work! • Record reference information on each source.

Adapted from *Student Research Guide*, Toronto District School Board,2003

InfoSkill:
Legal and Ethical Use of Information and Ideas
Students will understand copyright and use information ethically and legally.

Skill Discussion

In order to develop a respect for copyright, students must first understand the role fair laws play in supporting creators so that they have the means to continue to create and produce new products. Having done this we can begin to work on developing academic honesty.

To Ensure Academic Honesty
- Develop an awareness of copyright.
- Design information tasks that require students to construct meaning rather than regurgitate.
- Value the process as well as the product.
- Develop note-making skills.
- Teach referencing skills.
- Provide students with tools and strategies such as source sheets, referencing samples.
- Teach time management and organizational skills related to research projects.
- Develop a code of conduct for using information

Link Up

- Plagiarism: What it is and how to recognize and avoid it
  http://www.indiana.edu/~wts/wts/plariarism.html/

- Plagiarism Q and A
  http://www.ehhs.cmich.edu/~mspears/plagiarism.html

- How Not to Plagiarize
  http://www.utoronto.ca/writing/plagsep.html

- Copyright Board of Canada http://www.cb-cda.gc.ca/

- United States Copyright Office
  http://www.loc.gov/copyright/

Novice: *Explore Copyright Laws*

Teach through the Arts

To appreciate the arts is to enjoy and fully respect the creation and ownership of original thought. To broaden student understanding of the importance of copyright, ask them to assemble a collection of items that bear a copyright symbol or other notation of exclusivity. After a period of time instruct students to sort and categorize their artifacts. Discuss the broad range in types of items and develop a set of inquiry questions to frame further investigation.
- *What is copyright?*
- *Are there laws about copyright?*
- *What happens if you don't obey copyright?*
- *What is protected by copyright?*
- *Why is copyright important?*
- *What would happen without copyright laws?*
- *Does copyright apply to the Internet?*
- *What happens in other countries?*

Discuss with students how they could find answers to their questions e.g. books, articles, Internet, interviews with authors and artists, contact a publisher or producer etc.

Gathering Evidence of Understanding

Apply the jigsaw strategy for researching questions about copyright. Establish home groups, number off students and move to expert groups. Assign each expert group two questions to research. After a designated time period instruct students to move back with their home groups to share their findings. In the home group each students should be able to share accurate findings regarding the assigned question(s). Instruct each group to apply their collective knowledge and to create an informative pamphlet about copyright. With their permission, make copies to hand out to the rest of the student body.

Adaptation

Encourage students to always sign their own work. Purchase a copyright stamp for younger students. Insist on original work in all projects. To ensure students have a full appreciation of the ubiquitous nature of copyright, take this opportunity to work with fellow teachers to identify the role of copyright as it applies to the "real world" aspects of their subject areas e. g. rights to perform a play, to copy sheet music, to propagate plants, etc.

Apprentice: *Understand Referencing Formats*

Teach through English

Students are to critique a poem and use at least three professional reviews to substantiate their own thoughts. Provide students with samples of different kinds of citations and referencing e.g. in text, footnotes, works cited lists etc. Have students work in groups to examine the samples and prepare for a large group discussion based on the following questions:

- *What common information is found in all referencing styles?*
- *What is unique to each style?*
- *How does referencing change with each type of format?*
- *Why is referencing important to school projects?*

Review the skills of summarizing, paraphrasing, and note-making. See Note-Making Techniques, Fig. 29, also Fig. 28. Provide students with generic source sheets, such as Log of Sources, Fig. 11, to be kept in their research folder along with samples of referencing for every type of source.

Gathering Evidence of Understanding

Set up peer editing of poetry critiques. Students should be able to apply the referencing style requested and assess the accuracy of citations and referencing. Demonstrate the value of referencing as a component of the research process. Include referencing in the marking scheme.

Adaptation

Decide on standards for referencing as a school community. Remember to keep the standards developmentally appropriate. Systematically ensure that all classes have specific instruction and practice in keeping source records and documentation for citations and referencing by building these skills into unit and lesson planning.

InfoStar: *Proactive Strategies to Combat Plagiarism*

Teach through Literature

An independent novel study assignment requires that students read two novels and examine the expert reviews and analysis of the literature. They are to look for common themes and discrepancies. Based on this professional work students write an essay comparing the two novels. Take this opportunity to remind students about legal and ethical use of information. Have students brainstorm the reasons why some students plagiarize.

- misunderstanding or ignorance
- careless or poor note-making skills
- stress, competition, and lack of confidence
- poor time management and planning skills
- easy online access
- perceived cheating of others

Now assign each reason to a group of students. Instruct students to discuss strategies they could suggest to other students for avoiding both intentional and unintentional plagiarism.

Gathering Evidence of understanding

Share findings. Discuss and chart the suggested strategies. Then have the class design and produce a slide show that features their proactive ideas for combating the temptation to plagiarize. The slide show is to be shown to other classes and mounted on the school web page. Content of the slide show should demonstrate student understanding of the plagiarism avoidance strategies.

Adaptation

Design a workshop for teachers to explore ways of combating plagiarism. Have them brainstorm common reasons for academic dishonesty and in groups discuss proactive measures to ensure academic honesty. For ideas see *Legal and Ethical Use of Information (teacher prompts) Fig. 30, 31.*

Notes:
Reflect, Rethink, Redesign

√ Do students fully understand the need for copyright protection?

Documenting the Evidence

Teaching Unit Level
√ examine links between assignments and the occurrences of proper referencing and/or of plagiarism
√ design assignments to avoid invitational plagiarism
√ save and share exemplars
√ as a faculty, ensure students recognize and reference all types of information sources e.g. music, photographs, video, illustrations...
√ provide factual information and workshops on understanding legal and ethical use of information, for teachers, students and parents
√ provide easy access to current copyright information, for students, staff and parents

Legal and Ethical Use of Information (teacher prompts)

Why do students use information dishonestly?	What strategies can be provided for students and teachers to reduce the incidence of information dishonesty?
Misunderstanding or ignorance	• Review school/district code of conduct. • Inservice for staff/students and parents. • Teach information literacy skills and infuse in all curriculum. • Teach paraphrasing, summarizing quoting. • Provide readily accessible samples of documentation and citations. • Provide organizers to keep track of works consulted. • Reviewed and enforced by every subject/ discipline. • Prepare a "HELP" tool for students with definitions and contact information for assistance.
Careless or poor note-making skills	• Teach note-making techniques. • Provide students with visual organizers. • Teach students how to design visual organizers. • Teach students how to use technologies effectively for note-making. • Teach strategies that require students to think about the notes they are making and make connections. • Model making notes or provide examples. • Assess point form notes and visual organizers.
Stress and competition	• Provide students with time management training and strategies. • Invite students to participate in setting dues dates. • Conference with students throughout the process. • Include students in the design of assessment criteria. • Provide students with agendas and workshops in effective planning. • Coordinate major projects and assignments school wide. • Post student assignments electronically.
Poor time management and planning skills	• Emphasize time management and planning skills. • Use daily/weekly/monthly planners. • Dramatize time management juggling scenarios. • Build in writing time for assignments in class. • Design a series of process checkers/contracts. • Provide real life examples to demonstrate how critical these skills are. • Include parents in the design of solutions.

Lack of confidence	• Set up peer conferencing and mentoring sessions • Chunk the project into manageable sections • Provide more regular feedback • Value the process not just the product • Encourage students to ask for help • Ensure that everyone understands the assessment criteria • Share exemplars so students know what they are aiming for
Perceived cheating of others (students and adults)	• Don't give the same assignment year after year • Model academic honesty (credit quotes, ideas of others) • Always use media legally • Seize the teachable moment and discuss legal and ethic use of information when infractions occur at school and in the community • Be consistent and fair about consequences • Make consequences clear to all
Low level assignments (no critical thinking required)	• Design assignment that require students to construct personal meaning • Design performance assessment tasks that are real world situations • Structure the assignment so students have to analyze, synthesize and evaluate information • Teach students how to develop good inquiry questions and develop a theses statement if required • Become savvy of the indicators of plagiarism
Assessment of product only	• Value all stages of the assignment and provide feedback at every stage • Work with students to develop criteria for assessing process and product • Have students keep research portfolios and learning logs • Collect exemplars of student process as well as products

Adapted from Toronto District School Board with permission

Legal and Ethical Use of Information (Fig. 31)

Why do students use information dishonestly?	What strategies can be provided for students and teachers to reduce the incidence of information dishonesty?
Misunderstanding or ignorance	
Careless or poor note-making skills	
Stress and competition	
Poor time management and planning skills	

Lack of confidence	
Perceived cheating of others (students and adults)	
Low level assignments (no critical thinking required)	
Assessment of product only	

Notes:

Part 4: Analyze

The process of analyzing information requires both hands-on and minds-on activity. Students sort, organize, reorganize, look for connections, patterns and trends. They reflect on what they have discovered to make relationships and inferences. Students study cause and effect and discover how they relate to impact. This is the meaning making stage of research. Provide students with lots of opportunities to muck about with the information they have gathered, think about it, reflect, and talk to others about their discoveries.

(p90)	**Use Organizers**
	Novice: Simple Organizers
	Apprentice: Comparisons
	InfoStar: Design an Organizer
(p94)	**Sort**
	Novice: Chronological Sort
	Apprentice: Sort by Attribute
	InfoStar: Complex Sort for Evaluation
(P98)	**Compare**
	Novice: Teacher Criteria
	Apprentice: Student Criteria
	InfoStar: Student Criteria and Organizing Tool
(P102)	**Classify**
	Novice: Develop Categories through Manipulation
	Apprentice: Develop Categories through Experimentation
	InfoStar: Develop Categories and Systems
(p108)	**Identify and Investigate Patterns and Trends**
	Novice: Identify Patterns
	Apprentice: Identify Patterns and Trends
	InfoStar: Predict Trends
(p112)	**Respond to Text**
	Novice: Discuss and Illustrate
	Apprentice: Represent Visually
	InfoStar: Reflect and Question
(p116)	**Make Connections**
	Novice: Within a Single Text
	Apprentice: Multiple Texts
	InfoStar: Prior Learning, Other Disciplines
(p120)	**Cause and Effect**
	Novice: Discover Effect
	Apprentice: Determine Cause
	InfoStar: Analyze Cause and Effect
(p124)	**Impact**
	Novice: Examine Effect to Discover Impact
	Apprentice: Examine Perspectives to Determine Impact
	InfoStar: Evaluate Effects to Determine Impact
(p130)	**Interpret, Infer, Predict**
	Novice: Interpret
	Apprentice: Infer
	InfoStar: Predict
(p136)	**Understand Perspective**
	Novice: Identify Perspective
	Apprentice: Consider Perspective
	InfoStar: Gain Insight
(p140)	**Collaborate**
	Novice: Brainstorm Questions
	Apprentice: Test Ideas
	InfoStar: Electronic Communication

InfoSkill:

Use Organizers
Students will use graphic organizers to help analyze and synthesize data.

Skill Discussion

Graphic organizers are very useful processing tools. Like any other tools students need to be taught how to use them. Then they need to be given the support to adapt, modify and ultimately create their own.

Using graphic organizers helps students to break data apart for analysis. Similarly strategically designed templates can help students to work with data and build personal meaning. All templates need to be modeled in familiar contexts and applied repeatedly so students learn how and when to use each.

Use graphic organizers to help students:
- sort facts into categories
- compare and contrast information
- classify information
- distinguish between fact and fiction
- determine relationships
- display a sequence of events
- display connecting ideas
- identify cause and effect
- draw conclusions
- and ...

Link Up

- The Graphic Organizer www.graphic.org

- The Write Design www.writedesignonline.com/organizers/

- Inspiration Software www.inspiration.com

- Buehl,David. 2001. *Classroom Strategies for Interactive Learning*. Neward, DEL: International Reading Association.

- Hyerle,David. 1996.*Visual Tools for Constructing Knowledge*. Alexandris,VA: ASCD

- Koechlin, C. and Zwaan, S. 1997.Teaching *Tools for the Information Age*.Markham, ON:Pembroke

Novice: *Simple Concepts*

Teach through Language Arts

In the early years, use tactile methods to organize familiar objects such as crayons, beads, vegetables and clothing. Then progress to organizing information. Try using:
- Boxes, bowls and place mats for sorting.
- Hula-hoops for comparing
- Beads and string for beginning, middle, end
- Picture frames or styrofoam trays for sequencing

Then introduce various ways to organize information by paperfolding. Read great picture books and follow up with extensions that require organization of required data.
- Fold in half for sorting.
- Fold in three for classifying.
- Make an accordion fold for sequencing.
- Cut a circle and fold in four for cycles.
- Fasten three squares together for charting beginning, middle, and end.

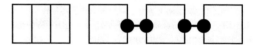

Give students lots of practice and keep paper organizers available for students to use independently.

Gathering Evidence of Understanding

Ask students to articulate their actions and thoughts as they work to organize objects and information. They should be able to record desired information accurately on the organizer in pictures and words. Students should use words like sort, chart, and organize to explain what they have done.

Adaptation

Organizing using these tactile strategies enables special needs learners to achieve.

Apprentice: *Complex Concepts*

Teach through Science

Students are required to compare two celestial objects. Model the process. Use short excerpts from non-fiction text and video clips to quickly give students background information about two celestial objects. e.g. Earth's moon and an asteroid. Record the information discovered on a T-Chart. Discuss with students to determine what would be important to compare. Develop comparison criteria and record it on a chart e.g. location, formation, physical properties, movement etc. Using a large chart or projection, develop a Venn. Take one criteria at a time and identify, then list similarities in the center where the circles overlap. Next, identify the differences with respect to those criteria, and record them in the appropriate circle sections. Discuss why this comparison is important and how this information could be used.

Gathering Evidence of Understanding

Have students work with a partner to select and compare two celestial objects. Instruct students to record their findings on a Venn. Ask them to conference with another pair and discuss the significance of their findings. Students should apply criteria for comparison and accurately plot similarities and differences.

Adaptation

Always model the use of new organizers. Prepare transparent overlays of graphic organizers at several stages of completion. Layer these overlays to teach and review the process of using different kinds of graphic organizers (see Fig. 32).

InfoStar: *Design an Organizer*

Teach through Social Studies

Students have been asked to chart the similarities and differences between a day in the life of a child in medieval times to their own day. After students have gathered their data, provide them with a thumbnail of an organizer and let them reproduce it and modify it to meet their needs. Teach students how to make effective use of draw tools to create their own organizers on the computer.

Gathering Evidence of Understanding

Have each student conference with a partner and discuss their organizers and their effectiveness. Students must be able to articulate the criteria they used for comparison and tell how they adapted the suggested organizer to meet their needs.

Adaptations

As curriculum standards dictate more advanced concepts such as cause and effect, provide students with lots of thumbnails of organizers to chose from such as those on *Go Graphic*. Model the use of each type of organizer and then strive to have students select and design the best organizer for their purpose. Have them develop a personal collection of template files they can adapt. Some commercial graphic organizer software programs are available as well and provide some interesting enhancements such as the

capability to convert to outlines and import graphics and hypertext links.

Ultimately we want students to be able to make a conscious link between their purpose and the type of graphic organizer they need to produce. (Inspiration™ might be introduced)

Notes:
Reflect, Rethink, Redesign

√ What kind of learners do organizers help?
√ How can I develop and organize a bank of samples and blank outlines of organizers for students to use or refer to when creating their own?
√ Do I model the use of organizers in my teaching?
√ How can I make connections between the use organizers at school and real life applications? e.g. shopping lists, after school schedules, balanced meals, time management...

Documenting the Evidence

Learner Level
Understanding of Skill
√ recognizes the need/opportunity to utilize organizers as learning tools
√ selects an appropriate organizer
√ makes connections between the information need and the construction of effective organizers
√ utilizes appropriate technologies to use or design organizers

Understanding Curriculum Content
√ demonstrates achievement of key knowledge on quizzes and tests
√ demonstrates understanding of complex curriculum concepts

Teaching Unit Level
√ collaborates to design tasks that apply graphic organizers to process information
√ discusses effectiveness with other staff
√ sets goals for improvement
√ shares successes with other staff members

Notes:

GO Graphic (Fig. 32)

Graphic organizers are useful visual tools to help you process the data you have gathered.

Use them to build personal meaning:
- **sort** facts into categories or sub-topics
- display a **sequence** of events or procedures
- **compare** and contrast information
- identify **connect**ing ideas
- **distinguish** between fact and opinion
- **analyze** conflicting information
- **identify** bias and perspective
- identify cause and effect
- **determine** relationships

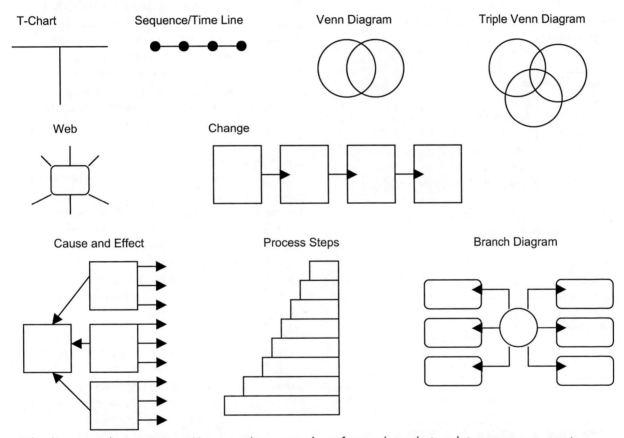

Why do you need an organizer? You can ask your teachers for ready-made templates or you can create your own on the computer using draw software. Make use of shapes, arrows, shading and color. Try out some ideas and make sketches of your own design. **Which organizer is best for your need? Why?**

Adapted from *Student Research Guide*, Toronto District School Board

InfoSkill:
Sort
Students will sort gathered data for specific purposes.

Skill Discussion

Sorting is an important entry-level analysis skill. Provide students with tactile/concrete sorting experiences before tackling the sorting of data e.g. sort pictures, books, stamps, etc.

Before students begin to sort anything, clear purpose and criteria must be established. You can help students with sorting by providing them with some thinking prompts.

Sorting Tips
- What am I sorting?
- Why am I sorting it?
- How will I organize things?
- Which relationships are important?
- What patterns am I looking for?
- Is there a better way to sort?
- How can I keep a record of my work?

That's Good; That's Bad	
That's Good	Why?
That's Bad	Why?

Link Up

- Sifting and Sorting Through Information
  http://www.bcps.org/offices/lis/models/tips/sift.html

- Koechlin, C and Zwaan, S.2001.*InfoTasks for Successful Learning*. Markham, ON: Pembroke Publishers

- Marzano, Robert et al.2002.*Handbook of Classroom Instruction that Works*. Alexandria, VA:ASCD

Novice: *Chronological Sort*

Teach through Social Studies

Students are learning about the diversity of their community. Send home a letter with students asking parents and caregivers to help students record significant events they observe throughout the year, including birthdays and family celebrations such as Chinese New Year and Kwanza, school holidays, school bookfair, recitals, parades, track and field day, etc. Provide a form so students will record accurate dates. Organize the gathering of more primary data from the school office and local community organizations. Have students record each event, including the date(s), on card stock and add illustrations or scanned pictures. Create a giant "yearline" in the school hall. Attach vertically, narrow strips of paper above and below the timeline, staggered to mark days of each month. Instruct students to sort their events chronologically. Have students attach their cards, in appropriate order, to the vertical strips.

Gathering Evidence of Understanding

Students should be able to sort their events by month and date and attach them appropriately to the timeline. Invite small groups of students to walk the *School Community Yearline* and share significant events. After the walk and talk sessions hold a class debriefing and chart common understandings. Students should be able to articulate observations such as the month with the highest number of birthdays.

Adaptation

Students are investigating how each decade in the 20th century impacted on society. Group students by sub-topics to be examined e.g. technology, the arts, health, politics etc. Have students record and sort their gathered data chronologically for easier analysis across sub-topics.

Apprentice: *Sort by Attribute*

Teach through Science

In preparation for a comparison of planets in the earth's solar system, students have brainstormed a number of questions to guide their data searches. Individual students prepare an index card for each one of the questions. Each student selects a planet, locates good sources, and records data to address their questions. Instruct students to sort the discovered data by recording it on the appropriate index card.

Gathering Evidence of Understanding

Ask students to periodically review the data on their cards to confirm that they are recording only information that responds to the question and that they are finding enough data for each question. Observe students as they research and record. Ask them to explain what they are recording and why, to ensure that they are able to sort data by question focus.

Adaptation

Ensure that students use a variety of types of resources. Match students' reading levels to appropriate resources. Arrange learning buddies as necessary.

InfoStar: *Complex Sort for Evaluation*

Teach through Technology

Students are exploring the impact of modern technology on humans and the natural world. They have brainstormed a list of 20th- 21st century devices/inventions and sorted their chronological debuts in society. To discover the impact of specific technological devices, they will need to collect data and sort it into positive and negative effects. Model the process with a very current device such as the cell phone. Ask students to work in groups and list effect of cellphones on humans and the natural world. Instruct groups to sort the data into two columns for effects on humans and effects on the natural world. Remind students to think of all stakeholders and examine the issue from all relevant perspectives e.g. owner, family and friends, manufacturers, advertising companies, fellow patrons, etc. Share student findings. As students share, ask the class to decide if the effect was good or bad and why. Re-sort by recording this analysis on a chart (paper, overhead) similar to *That's Good That's Bad, Fig. 33.*

Gathering Evidence of Understanding

Instruct students to record in their learning log how the brainstorming and sorting process helped them develop understanding about the issue. Students will now be ready to select another modern device and, independently, go through the process modeled. Have students use the organizer *That's Good That's Bad* to sort and record their findings. Students must be able to sort the data by effects on humans and effects on the environment and then sort again to evaluate that impact.

Notes:
Reflect, Rethink, Redesign

√ Are students having difficulty deciding on which category data belongs in?
√ Are there occasions when the same data appears to belong in more that one place? How do they handle that?
√ Are they tempted to change/add categories?
√ Does new data sometimes change their opinion about categories previously assigned?
√ Where does the need for sorting skills occur in other curriculum applications?

Documenting the Evidence

Learner Level
Understanding of Skill
√ accurately sorts objects
√ sorts data using criteria
√ independently creates new/different criteria for sorting
√ explains rationale for sort
√ applies sorting strategies independently on other situations

Understanding Curriculum Content
√ identifies subtopics
√ organizes information in subtopics
√ discovers new/different relationships and connections
√ is aware of different aspects and perspectives
√ understands the breadth of the topic
√ is prepared to come to a conclusion, make a decision or a suggestion

Notes:

(Fig. 33)

That's Good ⇕ That's Bad

That's Good	Why?	That's Bad	Why?

My analysis

Adapted from Koechlin and Zwaan *Info Tasks for Successful Learning*, Pembroke Publishers 2001

InfoSkill:

Compare
Students will make comparisons to discover relationships in gathered data.

Skill Discussion

Making comparisons is actually a complex process. Students must first of all determine exactly what is being compared and why, then decide which aspects of the items they will examine for the purposes of comparison. Consequently they need at least two bodies of information and pre-determined criteria to help sort the points of comparison. Once sorted, they need to determine what is similar and what is different. Although requirement for this skill appears often in learning expectations it is rarely taught as a skill.

To teach it successfully:

- Model the process in many familiar contexts e.g. comparing seasonal clothing, comparing fast food chains, comparing a book to a film adaptation etc.
- Make the experience as tactile and visual as possible e.g. use sticky notes, index cards, color, shapes, hula-hoops, and graphic organizers.
- Provide students with thinking prompts to guide the process.
- Talk about the process and ask students to articulate what they are doing and why.
- Evaluate student success and set goals for improvement.

Link Up

- Exploring Language: Making Comparisons
  http://english.unitecnology.ac.nz/resources/resources/exp_lang/comparisons.html

- Compare and Contrast
  http://www.writedesignonline.com/organizers/comparecontrast.html

- Koechlin Carol and Zwaan, Sandi.1997.*Information Power Pack: Intermediate Skills Book*. Markham, ON: Pembroke.

- Marzano, Robert. et al. 2001. *A Handbook for Classroom Instruction that Works*. Alexandria VA. Association for Supervision and Curriculum Development.

Novice: *Teacher Criteria*

Teach through Social Studies

Students are studying the diversity of communities in their own country (e.g. farming, fishing, industrial, tourist, city, village, etc.) They will be asked to determine similarities and differences between their own community and another. Provide an experience to review their own community so all students will have some common understandings. Discuss and chart important aspects of the students' local community. Ask students to look for similar bits of information and begin to visually sort the ideas on the chart. Use different colored markers to circle similar items e.g. green for buildings, blue for transportation, red for environment, yellow for jobs, etc. Name the categories and explain that these are the things they will use to organize the comparison of their own community to another. Now model the process by charting the information about their community and another one already studied. Use a large copy of an organizer such as *What's the Same What's Different?* Fig.34. Discuss the process.

Gathering Evidence of Understanding

Provide students with blank copies of the organizer *What's the Same What's Different?* Students should accurately record the common criteria for comparison e.g. buildings, transportation, environment, jobs, recreation, etc. Instruct students to select a community to compare. Students should sort data by selected criteria before attempting to fill in the organizer. Students should record similarities in the middle column, and differences in the respective outside columns. They need to review the information they have charted to decide if they have enough information or do they need to go back to original sources for more data to round out their comparisons. When completed have students find a partner and explain their comparison chart. Students should be able to articulate the process and their findings.

Adaptations

Prepare a chart of thinking prompts for making comparisons. Display the chart and refer to it often when conferencing with students.

Tips for Making Comparisons
- What are you comparing? Why?
- Which parts are important to compare?
- Chart the characteristics or criteria to be used for comparison.
- Use a tool to help you sort your data (highlighters, sticky notes, index cards, graphic organizer)
- Find what is similar
- Find what is different
- Now organize your data.
- Study the similarities.
- Consider the differences.
- Can you draw any conclusions?
- What have you discovered?
- Why is it important?
- Share your discoveries.

In primary grades students may begin with very basic comparisons where they look at two simple things and make general comparisons e.g. a crayon and a marker. They would identify attributes that are the same and later look for differences. Even at this level students should consider their findings and come to a conclusion e.g. both crayons and markers come in lots of colors; however, crayons last longer.

Apprentice: *Student Criteria*

Teach through Science

To familiarize students with navigation and functionality of online encyclopedias, prepare a comparison experience. Inform students that they will be required to use online encyclopedias to discover current information about global warming. Their job is to determine what criteria they will use so that they can systematically make comparisons. They will then conduct a comparison using common search tasks and the organizer *What's the Same? What's Different?* (Fig. 34) Prepare a search task worksheet providing students with search terms and specific tasks. Instruct students to work in groups to discuss the tasks and the criteria they think will be important for comparing the online encyclopedias e.g. search tools, structure/navigation, visuals, related links, usability, saving/printing etc.

Gathering Evidence of Understanding

Students must establish criteria for comparison and complete both the information task worksheet and the comparison chart. Students should be able to articulate their findings to a peer. Debrief as a group and discuss why this learning exercise is important for future use of online encyclopedia.

InfoStar: *Student Criteria and Organizing Tool*

Teach Through Geography

Students are to compare the amounts and types of natural resources in different parts of the world and use this analysis to make some predictions about global economic and environmental patterns. Review *Tips for Making Comparisons.* Provide students with examples of a variety of graphic organizers (such as *Charting Comparisons, Fig. 35* or *Go Graphic Feg.32*) designed to organize and develop comparison relationships.

Gathering Evidence of Understanding

Students should develop criteria for analysis and design their own organizer to help them sort their information and share their comparison findings. Students will create a visual projection of their graphic organizer (scanned image, slideshow, overhead) and prepare a short report of their findings to be shared with the class. Chart common findings and discrepancies in reports. Discuss the implications of the student findings.

Notes:
Reflect, Rethink, Redesign

√ Do students recognize the purpose of identifying bodies of data and sorting them by categories before they attempt to make their comparisons?
√ Do some learners need assistance with identifying criteria/categories?
√ What real life examples would help students understand the relevance of this skill?

Documenting the Evidence

Teaching Unit Level
√ identification of curriculum standards that require comparisons
√ design of lead up lessons so that students collect and record the data they will require to make the comparisons
√ collection of student work throughout the process to provide future exemplars
√ evaluation of student success for several applications of the skill to identify progress

What's the Same? What's Different? (Fig. 34)

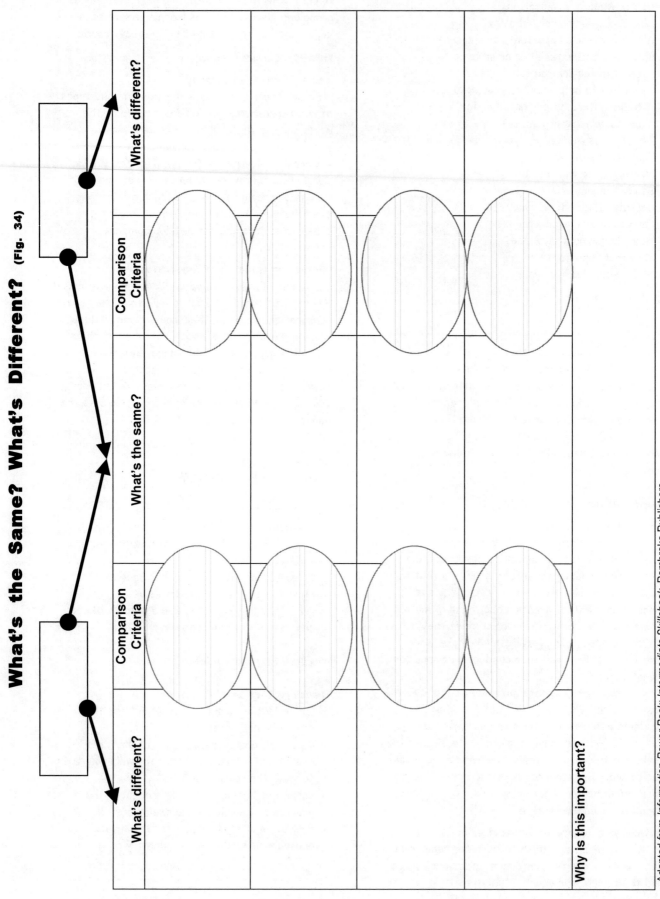

What's different?

Comparison Criteria

What's the same?

Comparison Criteria

What's different?

Why is this important?

Adapted from *Information Power Pack: Intermediate Skillsbook*, Pembroke Publishers

Charting Comparisons (Fig. 35)

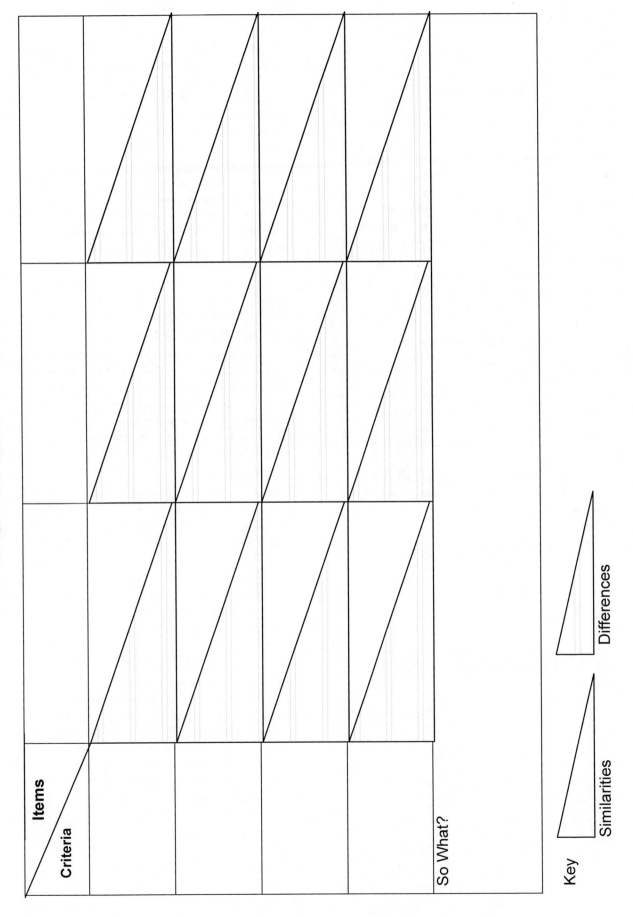

Items

Criteria

So What?

Key

Similarities

Differences

InfoSkill:

Classify
Students will classify data gathered for specific purposes.

Skill Discussion

Classifying formalizes the sorting process by applying a rule, a system or principle. This high level activity is a very important skill that information users need to understand. All information sources (e.g. non-fiction books, specialized encyclopedias, newspapers, videos, Web Sites etc.) are structured or organized using a system or principle. Experiences with sorting and classifying data will help students to understand how to find information when they need it.

To be successful in teaching students to understand sorting and classifying:

- Model the process in many familiar contexts e.g. classifying plants, buildings, musical instruments etc.
- Make the experience as tactile and visual as possible e.g. sticky notes, index cards, color, shapes, boxes, and graphic organizers
- Provide students with thinking prompts to guide the process.
- Talk about the process and ask students to articulate what they are doing and why.
- Evaluate student success and set goals for improvement.

Cross-Classification Chart, Fig. 36

Link Up

- Index - Graphic Organizers
  http://www.graphic.org/goindex.html

- Instructional Framework: Classifying Thinking Skill
  http://edservices.aea7.k12.ia.us/framework/thinking/classifying/

- Seaworld Adventure Parks: Diversity of Life
  http://www.seaworld.org/teacher-resources/guides/diversity-of-life/classifyit.html

Novice: *Develop Categories through Manipulation*

Teach Through Science

Prepare students for a study of animal types and habitats through background building activities using books, videos, excursions, etc. Group students and provide each student with a pile of sticky notes. Instruct students to brainstorm animals they know and recall animals they heard about in the exploration activities. Have each student individually record the name or make a sketch of one animal on each sticky note. Continue brainstorming as long as time allows. Provide each group with a large piece of chart paper. Ask students to share their animals, note duplicates and sort their animals by common habitat e.g. forest, desert, mountain, salt water etc. Have students move their sticky notes to the chart paper and create a chart or web of the classified animals. Instruct students to name each category.

Gathering Evidence of Understanding

Students should develop a complete chart/web with logical categories. Post charts/webs. Invite students to do a gallery walk to examine the work of each group. Have students make an entry in their learning logs reflecting on what they learned about animals and their habitats and how the process helped.

Adaptation

When students have learned about animal types, return to the displayed charts/webs and instruct students to classify the same animals by habitat and animal type. Prepare a large cross-classification chart, for a table or the floor, and have students lift their sticky notes from the charts/webs and remount them appropriately on the cross-classification chart.
Provide thinking prompts.

Tips for Classifying

- What needs to be organized? Why?
- Sort items looking for similar characteristics.
- Some items may fit in more than one place.
- Decide on the best fit for your purpose.
- Decide on a category name for each like group.
- Decide if some items fit in another category.
- What observations can you make?
- How will this organization help you?
- How can you use your chart/web?
- Share your discoveries.

Apprentice: *Develop Categories through Experimentation*

Teach through Geography

As a summative assessment task students are required to recall earth's surface features studied in previous classes e.g. mountain, island, stream, valley, bay, etc. They also have to develop a method to classify these earth formations. Provide students with the organizer *Classified* Information Fig. 37 as well as a copy of *Tips for Classifying*. Provide students with a rubric or other assessment criteria and ensure that everyone understands the task requirements.

Gathering Evidence of Understanding

Students must be able to name earth's surface features and also sort and classify them into logical categories. Observe students as they work and make anecdotal notes for reference when marking their tasks. Watch for and encourage experimentation with different categories and active sorting of features.

Adaptation

Use a teacher-prepared computer template or commercial software organization tool to make it easier for students to experiment with sorting and classification.

InfoStar: *Develop Categories and Systems*

Teach Through History

In preparation for an independent inquiry about individuals or groups who have contributed to their country's development, provide students with exploratory experiences e.g. pictures on a wall of fame, video clips, guided Internet searches, interviews with senior community members, etc. Group students and ask them to brainstorm a list of noteworthy groups and individuals. Post lists around the room. Invite groups to gallery walk to see each other's work and then retrieve their lists and continue brainstorming. Instruct students to now classify their lists. Remind students of *Tips for Classifying* and review some common organizer templates that might work e.g. *Classified Information* Fig. 37 and *Hierarchy Classification* Fig. 36. Invite students to adapt and modify the templates or to create their own template.

Gathering Evidence of Understanding

Learners must create/use an effective organizational tool that demonstrates the system they have applied for classification. Groups should be able to explain how they sorted and tested ideas to develop their system of organizing. Debrief and discuss how the process of classification will help students with their independent inquiries.

Notes:
Reflect, Rethink, Redesign

√ Do students make connections between the way things are classified and the attributes we tend to notice?

√ Are students able to see applications for this skill in everyday life?

√ Which students are having difficulty classifying? What other strategies could I use to help them?

√ Which students found the manipulation helpful?

√ Where could I apply this strategy to assist students in other learning experiences?

Documenting the Evidence

Learner Level
Understanding of Skill
- sort using criteria
- identify classifications logically according to purpose
- articulate reasoning for decisions

Understanding Curriculum Content
- improved ability to see relationships
- broader understanding of information being classified

Teaching Unit Level
- select other curriculum applications where students can practice this skill and record their success
- compare the results over time to determine which students have mastered it and which require remediation

Cross Classification Chart (Fig. 36)

Observations						
Questions						
Application						

Classified Information (Fig. 37)

Use this chart to help you organize the information you have gathered.
Sort the items you have by looking for similarities.

NOTE: The most important part of using this organizer is moving items around and experimenting with categories. When you have decided on the best way to sort establish a rule and name for each category.

Category Rule	Category Rule	Category Rule
Category Rule	Category Rule	Category Rule

How has classifying helped…..

What next?

Notes:

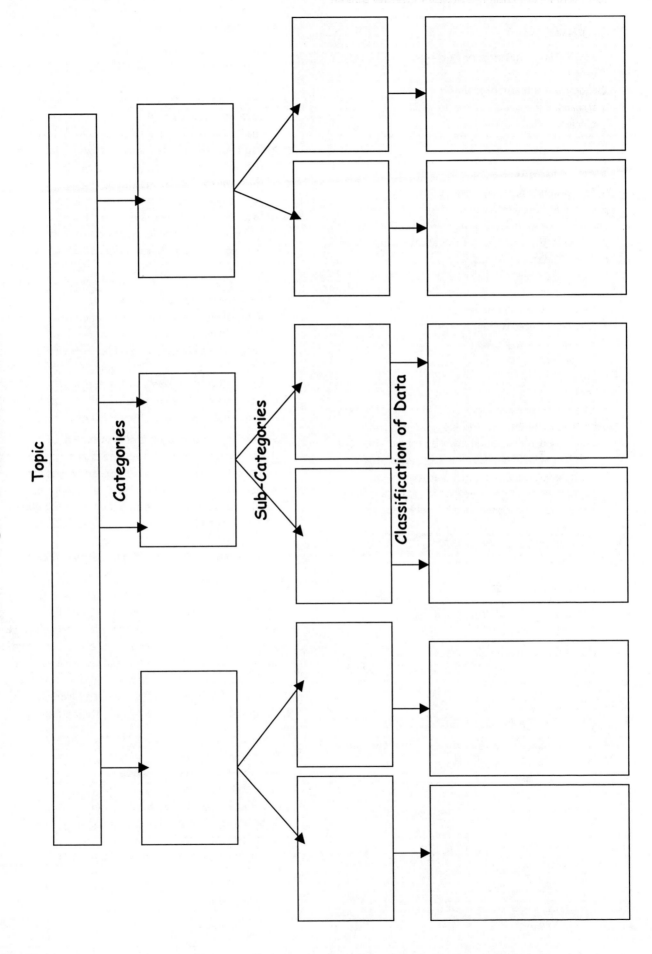

Hierarchy Classification (Fig. 38)

Topic

Categories

Sub-Categories

Classification of Data

InfoSkill:

Identify and Investigate Patterns and Trends
Students will identify and investigate patterns and trends related to their inquiries.

Skill Discussion

This skill is a pre-requisite for making predictions. Students will need lots of modeling and practice with identifying and investigating patterns and trends. Start with familiar patterns of similar ideas or things.

- repetitive events, characteristics, designs, routines
- historical events, timelines
- popular culture, fashion, music
- puzzles, games. jingles
- number patterns
- maps
- weather

When patterns are identified, look for trends over time. Students should learn to look for patterns and trends in all investigations. This skill has many specific applications e.g. media studies, literature, mathematics, weather, population growth, investigation of economic issues like supply and demand, trade, investment, marketing etc.

Link Up

- Teaching Media http://www.media-awareness.ca/eng/med/class/teamedia.htm

- Global Issues on the UN Agenda http://www.un.org/partners/civil_society/agenda.htm

- Global Issues http://usinfo.state.gov/topical/global/

- Global Trends 2015: A Dialogue About the Future With Nongovernment Experts http://www.odci.gov/cia/publications/globaltrends2015/

Novice: *Identify Patterns*

Teach through Literature

Begin teaching this skill with the familiar text of story.

- Read several storybooks with similar characters, settings, themes or illustrations and visually chart the similarities to show the patterns.
- Read several problem-based stories and chart the problem and solution ideas and the solution that works. Talk about the pattern.
- Read fairy tales. Look for patterns and discover together the elements of fairy tales.
- Analyze other familiar story types in the same way e.g. pour quoi tales, legends, tall tales, and fables.
- Investigate a poem or several poems of the same type for patterns.
- View films of the same genre and analyze them for patterns.
- Read several non-fiction books on a similar topic e.g. mice, cows, lions etc. Again ask students to help you find patterns in the types of information they contain. e.g. all the books tell about habitats, food, the young etc.

Gathering Evidence of Understanding

As students are selecting books for independent reading they should be able recognize and find series books. They should be able to make some predictions about books based on other similar books that they have read.

Apprentice: *Identify Patterns and Trends*

Teach through Health

Students will investigate healthy eating patterns. To begin they will conduct a survey to discover and analyze information about breakfast cereals. See *Design Surveys* p. 40 for more detailed instruction in teaching this strategy. Together with students, create a survey form. Instruct students to conduct the survey with several children and include a range of age groups in their sampling.

Name:..Age..............
Do you eat cereal?
What is your favorite cereal?
Why is it your favorite?
How did you first find out about this cereal?
Does anyone else in your family eat this cereal?
Does it offer a freebie?
How many types of cereal do you have at your home?

When surveys are completed form small groups and ask students to share their survey results. Instruct students to enter their results in a simple database or create charts. Use the database to create effective graphs. Ask students to look for patterns where there is identical repetition, as well as trends where the data shows a tendency. Share the group findings and discuss trends and patterns discovered.

Gathering Evidence of Understanding

Instruct each student to complete *Analyzing Patterns and Trends* Fig. 39. Students must identify patterns and trends and record some plausible reasons for them. They need to also record why this information is important to planning healthy diets. Upon completion have students share their analysis with a partner. Debrief as a class and record common understandings on a chart.

Adaptation

Have students gather cereal advertisements over a period of time. Study the advertisements in relation to the survey results. Help students to make connections between brand marketing and consumer habits.

Ask students to bring empty cereal packages. Read the ingredients and note the nutrition information for the cereal alone as well as with milk. Discuss the nutritional value of the cereals. Have students cluster the cereals by nutrient value. Again compare this analysis with the popularity survey and the advertising data. What do wise consumers need to think about when making purchases?

InfoStar: *Predict Trends*

Teach through Global Issues

Students will investigate future trends related to world issues. To introduce the topic and concepts to be examined read *If the World Were a Village: a book about the world's people in 2002* by Davis J. Smith. This powerful picture book is suitable for adolescents as well as younger children. Debrief the issues in the book by charting the topics and major current findings that relate to the village of 100. Dramatize some of the findings by having students represent groups of people and their plight in the global village to create a tableau.

Have students form groups and select an issue to investigate e. g population, food, water, education, environment etc. Add other issues that are relevant. Students need to develop a research plan and gather relevant data. Provide students with some prompts to help with the analysis of their data.

Tips for Identifying Patterns and Trends
What information is similar, related, or repeated?
How does...............relate to ....?
How is...................similar to...........................?
Is there a repeated pattern?
What is the reason for the pattern?
Does the pattern hold over time to develop a trend?
Do trends change? What is the rate of change?
Why would someone want to know this?
Why might a trend change?
Can you make some predictions based on the patterns and trends you have discovered?
What questions do you have about what you observed?

Gathering Evidence of Understanding

Each group will write a page for a class book entitled *If the World Were a Village: a book about the world's people in 2027.* Groups must analyze their data to discover patterns and trends and apply that analysis to create a page for the book. Publish the book and share it with other classes.

Notes:
Reflect, Rethink, Redesign

√ Would keeping an ongoing list of patterns and
√ trends help students become more aware of where they occur in daily life?
√ How else can I provide opportunities for students to practice this skill?

Documenting the Evidence

Learner Level
Understanding of Skill
√ identifies patterns in a variety of settings
√ identifies repeated patterns
√ discovers tendencies and trends
√ notices change over time
√ notices rate of change
√ predicts trends

Understanding Curriculum Content
√ explains the pattern/trend in the context of the content
√ predicts future situations based on patterns or trends

Notes:

Analyzing Patterns and Trends (Fig. 39)

Look over the data you have gathered. Record any patterns or repeated information e.g. seasonal exports over a period of time, target advertising on television stations.

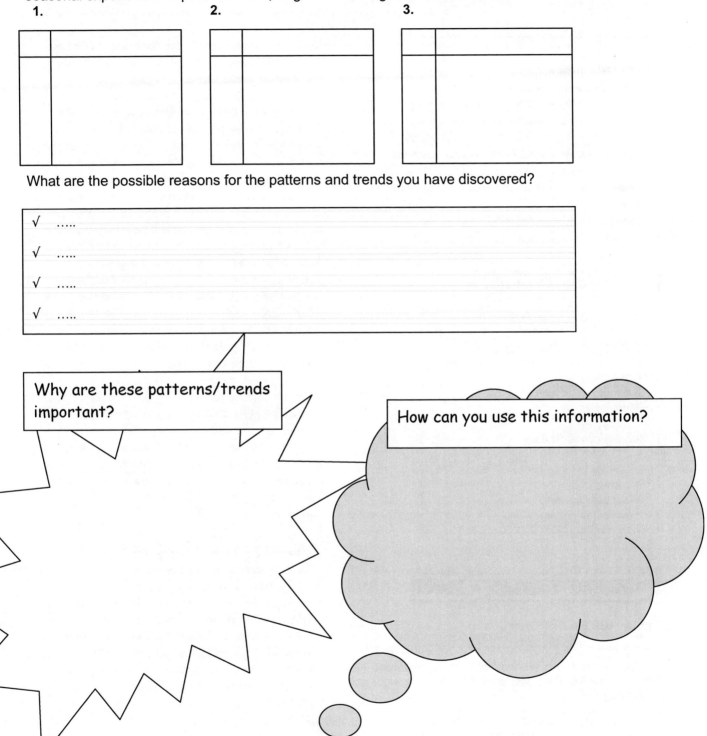

1.

2.

3.

What are the possible reasons for the patterns and trends you have discovered?

√ .....

√ .....

√ .....

√ .....

Why are these patterns/trends important?

How can you use this information?

InfoSkill:

Respond to Text
Students will analyze an information text by reacting to the data on a personal level.

Skill Discussion

As students read, view, and listen to the information, they need to be actively engaged. They need to learn how to process information by responding to it and interacting with it. Help students to make connections between what they see, hear or read and what they already know. Provide students with a variety of strategies so that eventually they will be able to self-select the strategies that are most effective for the information they are working with.

Working with Information

- Establish your information need.
- Collect the best resources.
- Actively read, view, listen.
- Select and record relevant information.
- Cite your sources.
- Rework information visually.
- Think about it.

Recording and Seeing
.....

Thinking
- What does it mean?
- Why is it important?

Link Up

- Koechlin, Carol and Zwaan, Sandi. 2001. *Info Tasks for Successful Learning: Building Skills in Reading, Writing and Research.* Markham, ON: Pembroke Publishers

- Harvey, Stephanie, 2000. *Strategies That Work: Teaching Comprehension to Enhance Understanding* York, Maine: Stenhouse Publishers

Novice: *Discuss and Illustrate*

Teach Through Science

Model the inquiry skills of identifying information needs and actively reading, listening and viewing to discover relevant data as the students are beginning an investigation of animal survival. Use a classroom pet or borrowed one to provide the optimum learning experience for students. Provide an overall inquiry question to frame the lesson(s). e.g. *How do gecko lizards survive in their environment?* Discuss the terms "survival" and "environment". Have students suggest questions they need to ask to find out about the survival of gecko lizards. Put the questions on the left column of a T-Chart leaving ample room on the right to record information discovered later. Select two or three non-fiction books and explain to students that these books are not storybooks but that they are information books that will help them answer some of their questions. Demonstrate how to use special features of non-fiction books to find specific information. As you read sections of text invite students to react when they hear something that answers one of their questions. Record the data on the T-Chart immediately. Encourage them to reflect on the findings and discuss ideas they have that relate to the finding.

Then review the questions and arrange for the students to take turns observing the gecko in the classroom. Have students make sketches of physical and behavioral characteristics that help the gecko to survive in its environment. If a live gecko is not available provide students with a short video and show them how to pause or stop and rewind as necessary and then sketch their discoveries.

Gathering Evidence of Understanding

Make up a mini information book for each student entitled *How do gecko lizards survive in their environment?* Instruct students to select from their sketches those that best represent the gecko's survival techniques. Students glue these in their books, adding text when possible. Invite students to share their findings in small groups. They should be able to show their illustrations and tell about the gecko's special features and the abilities that help it survive.

Adaptation

This skill of reacting to the text while actively engaging in reading, viewing and listening should also be applied to the study of fiction, poetry, songs, television programs, special guests, etc.

Apprentice: *Represent Visually*

Teach Through Language

In preparation for a current events project students will read selected newspaper articles, listen to, and view news reports. Remind students that active reading, viewing and listening means paying full attention to the text, visuals, and sound, and reacting to it. Provide students with tips to prompt their response.

Tips for Responding to Text
• Read, view, listen
• Identify the main points
• Develop mental pictures
• Record in point form
• Make the information visual
• Make sketches charts diagrams, webs, graphs, maps, etc.
• Connect to what you already know
• Ask questions

Give students the organizer *Working with Information* Fig.40. Demonstrate using the organizer to respond to a print and to a taped news article.

Gathering Evidence of Understanding

Each student selects a news text and follows the prompt tips to complete the organizer *Working with Information* Fig. 40. Students share their response sheets in small groups. They should be able to discuss the main points of the news item and explain why the item is important. Students in the role of listener should also use the tips to react and respond, to explanations of why the event is important.

InfoStar: *Reflect and Question*

Teach Through Economics

Students are required to select an imported fruit or vegetable and investigate the path it has traveled from seed to the table. Instruct students to examine all related issues in the global marketing of this product e.g. working conditions of laborers, packaging, advertising, transportation, trade agreements etc. Have students keep a reflective log of their personal reactions to the data they gather and the questions that they have with regard to the impact of the global marketing of this produce.

Gathering Evidence of Understanding

Students will produce an interactive flowchart of the path of the produce. Each step of the process should link to:
• questions raised by the learner during their investigation
• personal connections and student reactions
• hyperlinks to related websites

Notes:
Reflect, Rethink, Redesign

√ How does discussion with other students affect student interpretation of the findings/issues?
√ How can I ensure that students are discovering all relevant perspectives involved in individual issues?
√ What could I do to make student discussions more effective?

Documenting the Evidence

Learner Level
Understanding of Skill
√ focuses on the media item
√ accurately identifies required information
√ reflects on found data
√ makes comments or asks questions related to found information
√ creates appropriate sketches, charts, maps etc.
√ reacts to findings
√ questions, applauds, criticizes, evaluates findings

Understanding Curriculum Content
√ explains information to others in a meaningful way
√ discusses topic knowledgably
√ asks relevant questions
√ makes personal connections

Notes:

Working with Information (Fig. 40)

Name _____

- Establish your information need.
- Collect the best resources.
- Actively read, view, listen.
- Select and record relevant information.
- Cite your sources.
- Rework information visually.
- Think about it.

Recording-point form notes and data	Seeing-web, graph, sketch

Thinking
What does it mean?
Why is it important?

Adapted from *InfoTasks for Successful Learning*, Pembroke Publishers 2001.

InfoSkill:

Make Connections
Students will work with information to make connections.

Skill Discussion

Just as we help students make meaning when reading fiction, we need to structure similar activities to help them build connections as they read, view, listen to non-fiction text. There are many "connection building" strategies we can teach to help students understand content. When we suggest that students make connections we want them to make links to what they already know. What they know about the topic, what they know about reading (viewing/listening) strategies, what they know about webbing/mapping, and how this new content fits into their personal experiences. While we can contribute to background knowledge by providing a learning experience, such as an on topic video to level the playing field, students will all bring something different to the topic. To capitalize on these student experiences try the ideas suggested in *Connecting with Content*.

Connecting with Content

- Think about a similar situation, event, place etc.
- Develop an analogy.
- Paraphrase the text.
- Make a visual of the information.
- Record reflections on stickie notes.
- Develop questions about the content.
- Talk to a learning buddy about something that surprises you, or puzzles you.
- Record key points you have learned.
- Make a web of connections discovered.
- Draw a sketch representing the content.

Lots of discussion about the topic will help students to verbalize their thoughts. Hearing ideas, experiences, and connections of other students will add to their understanding of the topic.

Link Up

- Content Reading
http://www.content-reading.org/

- Reading Quests
http://curry.edschool.virginia.edu/go/readquest/links.html

- Improving Student's Understanding of Textbook Content
http://www.ldonline.org/ld_indepth/teaching_techniques/understanding_textbooks.html

- Harvey, Stephanie, 2000. *Strategies That Work: Teaching Comprehension to Enhance Understanding* York, Maine: Stenhouse Publishers

Novice: *Within a Single Text*

Teach through the Arts

Discover how the work of major impressionist artists contributed to cultural development. e.g. Monet, Degas, Renoir, Pissarro

The overall information quest for the class has been introduced. Through exploratory experiences students have discovered the names of major artists of the period. Each student will now select an artist they are interested in and then search for a suitable print resource. Once they have selected a resource, provide students with different colored sticky notes, or different colored pencils/pens. Instruct them to use one color note for thoughts /reflections about the text, another color for surprises or discoveries they make, and a third color for questions they have as they read.

Gathering Evidence of Understanding

Have students who have investigated different artists, assemble in groups of four or five after they have read one text and made their connections. Direct your students to work in small groups to share the notes they have recorded in the various colors.

Instruct them to look for links, similarities, relationships..., and note any connections they can make among the lives of individual artists. Have students chart the connections they discover. Allow them time to discuss the discoveries they made and as well as their personal reflections and questions. As you debrief students should begin to discover not only the contributions of individual artists but also the contributions made collectively, as a group, by these artists.

Adaptation

Model this experience for young researchers. Read a text out loud from a non-fiction Big Book. As you read, think out loud and record your thoughts, discoveries, and questions on large sticky notes and fasten them to the appropriate place in the text. You may want to introduce icons for each type of connection.

Thoughts/reflections
I wonder…..
Perhaps…..
Surprises/Discoveries
I discovered…
I learned….
Questions
 Who, What, When, Where
Why, How

Apprentice: *Multiple Texts*

Teach through History

Students are preparing to investigate the historical significance of *The Underground Railroad*. They will read picture books such as *Barefoot: Escape on the Underground Railroad* by Deborah Hopkinson and *Sweet Clara and the Freedom Quilt* by Pamela Duncan Edwards. Students will view videos and read selections of non-fiction text. As they work with each text they will record key information bits about events, people, experiences, locations and issues. Use different colored highlighters to identify commonalities in the information bits. Have students use the organizer, *All Things Connected* Fig. 41 to record the connections they make between texts.

Gathering Evidence of Understanding

Students should be recording commonalities, as well as differing and conflicting data from all of their sources. Have students share their findings with a learning buddy to ensure that they made appropriate connections and uncovered all the relevant information.

InfoStar: *Prior Learning and Other Disciplines*

Teach through Dramatic Arts

Students are to dramatize material they have researched from primary sources e.g. historical documents, letters, diaries, photographs. Collectively the class will create a documentary that effectively depicts the period in history. Connect this task with a history topic the students are studying e.g. the industrial revolution, the great depression of the 30s, the Cuban missile crisis etc. Once students have located primary sources, instruct them to analyze these using *Analyzing Primary Sources* Fig. 19. Now students need to think about different dramatic forms e.g. role playing, mime, storytelling, readers theatre, freeze, etc. and make connections between these and their primary source to decide on the best drama form to most effectively convey the information they have discovered from their primary source.

Gathering Evidence of Understanding

Each student should find a primary source, analyze it, and select an appropriate drama form. They should plan and rehearse a dramatic presentation.

Lead the class through a process of planning the order of their docudrama so that it best captures a representation of the period. Afterwards have students record the personal reflections and connections they were able to make to the historical period.

Notes:

Reflect, Rethink, Redesign

√ Are students able to reflect, discover and ask useful questions?
√ How can I ensure that students have lots of opportunity for meaningful talk to help them see the links?

Documenting Evidence

Learner Level

Understanding the Skill

√ considers information in the context of previous learning or personal experiences
√ questions, reflects on information
√ makes discoveries
√ identifies similar or related issues, situations, experiences
√ links new information to previous learning and/or personal experience
√ describes issue, experience, event with clarity

Understanding Curriculum Content

√ understands events and issues rather than simply memorizing facts about them
√ imagines oneself in the situation, event
√ empathizes with key players
√ links learning to other situations and applies new skills and knowledge

Notes:

All Things Connected (Fig. 41)

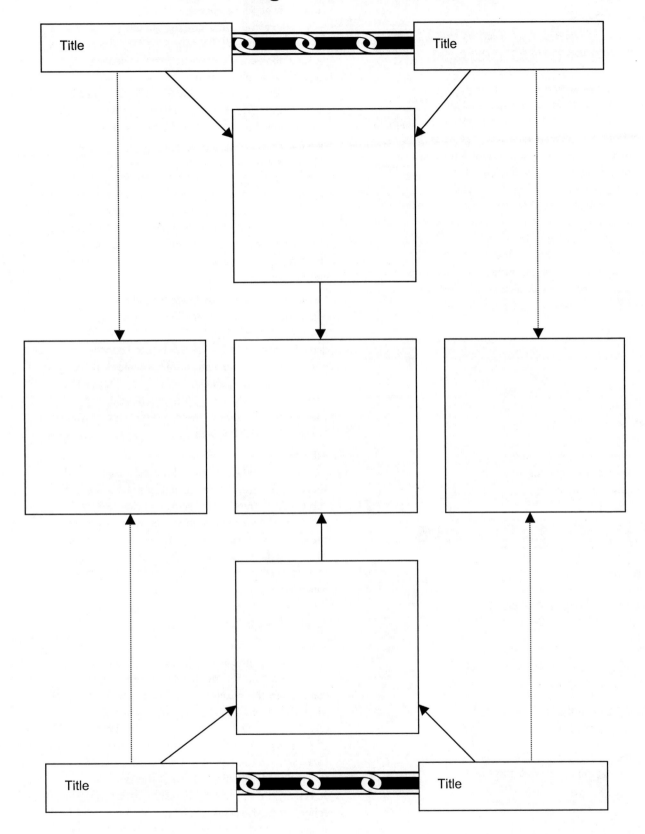

InfoSkill:
Cause & Effect
Students will work with information to determine cause and effect relationships.

Skill Discussion

Cause tells why something happens and effect tells what happens. Effects are pretty easy to pin down; however, determining causal relationships is much trickier because cause involves digging back into the past. One of the challenges with this skill is avoiding the effect of emotions and prior learning experiences. They can sway our thinking so that we jump to incorrect conclusions about causes of an event. Likewise, interpretation of the effect is subject to perspective. One also has to be careful of false cause and effect relationships, e.g. "It always rains when I wash my car" or "We always win the game when I wear my shirt inside out."

This skill is essential to help students analyze and develop understanding of complex information such as:
• social problems
• historical events
• conflicts
• current events
• catastrophes and disasters
• environmental changes
• economic patterns

Link Up

• The Fishbone Graphic Organizer
http://www.balancedreading.com/graphorg.pdf

• The Cause-Effect Essay
http://www.howard.k12.md.us/mth/english_dept/adv-comp/eng_effect.html

• Every Trick in the Book Week 15
http://www.cobbk12.org/~ar/week15.htm

• Bellanca, James. 1990. *The Cooperative Think Tank*. Arlington Heights Ill: SkyLight.

Novice: *Discover Effect*

Teach through Science

Introduce the focus question, How does human intervention affect environments? Read a powerful picture book about a change in an environment caused by people, such as *The World that Jack Built* by Ruth Brown or *The Great Kapok Tree* by Lynn Cherry. Identify the critical events e.g. building the factory and cutting down a tree respectively. Examine the illustrations, and discuss with students the effects these events had, or could have on the environment, and chart them. Look for commonalties and sort the effects into sub-topics e.g. animal life, plants and people. Instruct students to brainstorm words to describe a polluted river or a tree being chopped down. In small groups have student dramatize the polluted river or the dying tree.

Gathering Evidence of Understanding

Provide students with other scenarios e.g. a swamp is drained for development. Have students draw before and after pictures and record the effects of the event on the environment in thought bubbles. Students should be able to think of the effects on animal life, plants and people, and then show those changes in their illustrations as well as in their thought bubbles.

Adaptation

Older students studying about this topic could search the Internet for environmental sites both public and activist and discover actual events. They should gather information about the effects of the event from all relevant perspectives and work to form a personal opinion about what the effects of this event on the environment mean for the community.

Apprentice: *Determine Cause*

Teach through Science

In preparation for a study of pollution students are to determine some of the common causes of pollution in their community. Discuss with students what they know about pollution. Chart their ideas and then sort them into categories or broad types of pollution. Take an issue students are very familiar with such as litter in the schoolyard. Inform students that although the issue is pollution, the effect is the visible garbage in the schoolyard. The cause is not so obvious. Model for students how to backward map so that they can discover the critical event or cause of the current condition.

Determining the Cause

Articulate the Problem: Garbage is cluttering the yard. The custodial staff is spending too much time picking up. The yard always looks awful.

Articulate the Normal/Desired Condition
Litter should be deposited in containers provided and cleaned out frequently. Students should be responsible citizens.

Backward Mapping
Ask questions to set up the scenario that led up to the current problem and list the possibilities.
- What happened to garbage before the problem?
- When did the symptoms of this condition begin to appear?
- What changes occurred prior to that, which might have a connection to this problem?
- Why did these changes take place?

Evaluate Findings
Create a visual chart, timeline or other organizer for recording findings to help see connections and discover the causes of the schoolyard mess.

Form a Conclusion
e.g. Cause of Litter Problem
When containers were moved from near entrance doors to the perimeter of the yard to make curbside pickup of garbage and recycling more convenient for municipal workers, students gradually began to drop litter in the yard rather than be late entering after the bell.

Make Recommendations
Place small additional garbage containers by entry doors. These should be emptied into large street-side containers daily. Initiate a schoolwide awareness campaign to keep grounds clean.

Gathering Evidence of Understanding
Form five investigation teams. Each team will work together to determine causes for a type of pollution (air, water, land, sound, visual). Brainstorm with students some methods they can use to gather the causal evidence they need.
• Observe.
• Interview community members.
• Talk to an expert - health official, engineer, city planner...
• Take photographs and video/audio footage.
• Consult government organizations, environmental groups...
• Search local periodicals.
Provide students with the organizer *Determining the Cause* Fig. 42. They should work as a team

exploring sources and be able to complete the organizer ready for sharing.

Adaptation
Determining causal relationships is a logical science activity but it also transfers to well to literature. Every good picture book has an event or problem and every novel builds on many events and problems. Sometimes there is a single cause, sometimes there are many causes often taking place over time. The cause can be both explicit and implicit. Have students identify and record these causal relationships visually using shapes and arrows.

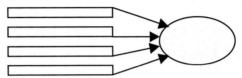

InfoStar: *Analyze for Cause and Effect*

Teach through History
Students are investigating the causes and effects of The Great Depression of the 30s. They are using a variety of resources; textbooks, encyclopedias, videos and other reference resources. Use a common text selection to model that some words and phrases are indicators of causes of an event and others are indicators of effects of an event. Chart these "indicator" words and phrases (e.g. because of, due to, consequently, hence, therefore, on account of, etc.) as students discover them.

Gathering Evidence of Understanding
Provide students with the organizer, *Investigating Cause and Effect* Fig. 43. Instruct students to record the causes and effects of The Great Depression. Remind students to look for the indicator words to help them uncover causes and effects. Remind them also to backward map to discover causes.

Notes:
Reflect Rethink, Redesign

Documenting Evidence of Understanding

Learner Level
Understanding of Skill
√ describes current situation
√ gathers data describing causes
√ makes connections between cause and effect
√ skims for "indicator words" to identify cause and effect relationships
√ applies backward mapping procedure to analyze a situation and discover the cause/s

Determining the Cause (Fig. 42)

The problem/event/issue

The normal/desired state

Backward Mapping - symptoms, timing, related changes...

N.B. Consider using the back of this sheet to make a chart, timeline, graph or other visualization of this scenario to help you evaluate your findings.

Evaluate findings and conclude

Recommend/predict

Investigating Cause and Effect (Fig. 43)

This organizer will help you to sort out the reasons some things happen as well as the consequences of an event. Use the connector words as clues to uncovering the causes and effects of an event.

Because..... Due to.....
As a result of...Since...
On account of.....
For this reason...
Leading to......

So... therefore.... Thus....
As a result.....Hence....
Consequently....
Resulting in....
With the result that....

Event

Causes

Effects

Now I understand that....

InfoSkill:

Impact
Students will analyze information to determine impact.

Skill Discussion

Impact is the collective forces or results of the cumulated effects of an event. Determining impact is a complex, multifaceted skill. Students must be able to first determine effects of an event, and then make sure they have examined all relevant perspectives to identify all those affected. They must be able to analyze for positive and negative spin-offs of the event. Finally students have to weigh all of this analysis, make links with other knowledge they have, and then evaluate the overall impact. This skill is imperative for working with any issues-based information.

Discovering Impact (Fig. 46)

• **Who/what was affected?**

• **How?**

• **What are the implications?**

• **In view of this information…**

Link Up

• Koechlin, C., & Zwaan, S. (2001). *Info tasks for successful learning: Building skills in reading, writing, and research.* Markham, ON: Pembroke.

• Zebra Mussel Distribution   http://www-atlas.usgs.gov/zmussels1.html

• The Zebra Mussel Page http://sun.science.wayne.edu/~jram/zmussel.htm#slide1

• Zebra Mussel Information http://nas.er.usgs.gov/zebra.mussel/

• Zebra Mussels in the Great Lakes http://www.great-lakes.net/envt/flora-fauna/invasive/zebra.html

Novice: *Examine Effects to Discover Impact*

Teach through Science

Students are investigating the interdependency of plants and animals of a specific habitat to each other. Read a picture book dealing with this issue such as *Wolf Island* by Cecila Godkin. Have students identify the event that broke the food chain, list the effects that resulted from that event, and the impact these effects had on the specific habitat, the island. Chart these findings as follows.

Wolf Island Events

First - wolf pack left the island

Then
• deer population increased
• deer ate all the vegetation
• no food for rabbits and mice
• vegetation sparse
• animals dying

Impact
• ecosystem is in danger

Follow with a short video dealing with a similar event. Again model the process of identifying the event, charting the chain of effects and determining the impact of the event on the habitat.

Gathering Evidence of Understanding

Select four stories or picture books similar to Wolf Island. Set up four workstations with copies of one of the texts at each station. Instruct students to work with a partner and read a story/book at each station, analyze the information and complete the organizer *Examining Chains of Effect* Fig. 44. Students should be able to identify and record the causal event, the chain of effects, the impact these had on the interdependency of plants and animals, and finally, the impact on the ecosystem.

Note: You will find that most of the stories and books resolve, or begin to resolve, the negative impact of the event e.g. In *Wolf Island* the wolves return to the island and balance is restored. You may want to instruct students to read only up to a certain point in some books and then read the remainder when they have completed the task.

Adaptation

This skill allows a natural and smooth transition from familiar fiction to non-fiction text. Provide students with opportunities to discover the chain of events in novels. Have them record effects of an event in the story on strips of paper and then glue these into circles and interlock to create a visual chain of effects. Then make the transition to newspapers, magazine articles and other non-fiction resources and apply the process with these.

Apprentice: *Examine Perspectives to Determine Impact*

Teach through Science

Students are examining the impact that the introduction of a foreign organism has on an ecosystem. Show a video clip that highlights the zebra mussel invasion of the *Great Lakes* system in North America. Invite students to share their personal knowledge about the rapid spread of zebra mussels. Use blank *Discovering Impact* organizer Fig. 45 or create a triple T-Chart labeled: Who /What was affected? How were they affected? What are the implications?

Fill in the chart with data gleaned from the video and student personal knowledge.
Have students work on selected Internet sites to discover more information about the zebra mussel invasion. Collaboratively complete the chart with students. Have students identify the variety of people/things affected. Discuss the consequences of these effects. See the organizer *Discovering Impact* Fig. 46

Gathering Evidence of Understanding

Provide students with other events where human intervention has impacted on an ecosystem e.g. mustard seed on the prairies, reintroduction of wolves in the West. Instruct them to investigate the issue and complete the organizer *Discovering Impact*. Students should be able to conduct the research and analyze their discoveries by identifying who/what was affected and how, as well as articulating the consequences of each identified effect. It is very important that students identify all of the relevant perspectives concerned.

Adaptation

Some students could extend and enrich this investigation by discovering the ripple effects of the implications.

InfoStar: *Evaluate Effects to Determine Impact*

Teach through History

Students have investigated causes and events leading up to the Cold War. They will now work in groups to discover the effects and ultimate impact of the Cold War. Brainstorm with students broad categories where they would expect to find fallout as a result of the Cold War e.g. world governments, politicians, culture, technology, economics, weapons industry etc. Instruct students to apply all their search skills and note-making skills to this task. Remind them also to make sure they use a broad range of validated sources.

Gathering Evidence of Understanding

Provide students with the organizer *Analyzing Impact* Fig. 47. Have students talk about the effects they have discovered while analyzing for positive and negative, short and long term effects. Students should be able to complete the organizer or create one of their own and identify the following: Who /what was affected? How were they affected? Will these effects have positive or negative impact? What will be the immediate impact? What will the long term effects be? What are the overall consequences?

Notes:
Reflect, Rethink, Redesign

√ Did students have sufficient background knowledge to work with these tasks?
√ Did students begin to empathize with some of the affected groups? Why or why not?
√ What effect does this have on the success of the learning experience?

Documenting the Evidence

Learner Level
Understanding of Skill
√ identifies initial event/s
√ lists effects and affected
√ articulates impact of effects
√ identifies perspectives of all affected
√ parties
√ discovers the consequences of the impact
√ evaluates the effect of the impact and its consequences

Examining Chains of Effects
(Fig. 44)

Impact

Chains of Effects

Event

Discovering Impact (Fig. 45)

Topic:..

Resource #	Who/what was affected?	How?	What are the implications?

In view of this information……..

Adapted from *InfoTasks for Successful Learning*, Pembroke Publishers 2001.

Discovering Impact (Fig. 46)

Topic: Zebra Mussels in the Great Lakes

Who/what was affected?	How?	What are the implications?
Boats-navigational and recreational	- mussels attach to hull and engine parts	- increased drag from weight - overheating of engine - damage to cooling system
Fishing gear	- fouled if left in the water too long	- damaged beyond repair - expensive to replace
Navigation buoys and docks	- mussels attach and weight them down	- become encrusted and sink - corrosion of steel - weakening of concrete
Beaches	- broken shells and foul smell	- ruins appearance - danger to bare feet
Native mussels	- attacked by zebra mussels - latch on to them	- interferes with feeding, growth, movement and respiration as well as reproduction - clams cannot open shells
Water supply pipes of hydroelectric and nuclear power plants Public water supplies Industrial facilities	- mussels attach and constrict flow	- reduced water intake and flow - damages fire fighting equipment - damages air conditioning and cooling systems - damages irrigation systems
Cottagers	- constant battle to keep lakes clean	- clogged water systems expensive to repair - damage to docks, boats and fishing gear sharp shells are dangerous - need to rinse boats all the time
Whitefish, sculpin, smelt, and chubb	- Starving because they cannot find - Diporeia, tiny shrimp-like crustaceans. - Diporeia loss is due to competition for algae with the zebra mussels	- loss to commercial fishing of whitefish and also trout and salmon which because the smaller fish are prey for them
Clarity of water	- mussels filter algae from the water turning it clear	- increased scuba diving on the great lakes now - increase in aquatic plants provides cover and nurseries for some new species of fish

In view of this information….

This invasion is a disaster for the great Lakes water system. The damage to the environment and industry is growing daily. The methods that have been tried to rid the lake of these pests have not been successful.
How valuable are the positive effects ?

Are boaters doing all they can to stop the spread of zebra mussels? Are people taking this problem seriously?
Surely scientists can do something before it is too late? What if the problem is never solved? We can't let zebra mussels spread to all the fresh water in North America.

Why can't a natural predator be introduced? Could a control area be set up to experiment with some natural solutions?

Analyzing Impact (Fig. 47)

What is the Event/Issue?

For who/what?	Positive effects	Not sure......	Negative effects	For who/what?

Short term impact

Long term impact

Overall I think......

InfoSkill:

Interpret, Infer, Predict
Students will interpret information to develop inferences and make predictions.

Skill Discussion

Analysis of data in the research process requires that students can take information they have gathered about their topic, examine it closely and develop personal understanding. They accomplish this by mentally and physically processing the gathered data.

To do this, they:

1) Interpret the meaning of the texts they are reading, viewing or listening to.

2) Make some inferences about the data based on text clues and prior knowledge and experiences. They apply both inductive and deductive reasoning to construct meaning beyond what is explicitly stated.

3) Apply their interpretation and inferences to making a personal prediction.

4) Work with others and test out their ideas and adjust analyses to clarify their understanding.

To infer is to extend information beyond what is explicitly stated. It is a process of reading between the lines, reasoning and making assumptions to arrive at a personal decision or conclusion. It involves the application of two reasoning skills.

- **Inductive reasoning** - analyzing data to draw conclusions.
AND/OR
- **Deductive reasoning** - taking a known idea or generalization and testing it out in a particular situation.

Link Up

- Teaching Inference, Interpretation and Analysis
http://www.fno.org/feb02/inference.html

- Cognitive Apprenticeship: Making Thinking Visible
http://www.21learn.org/arch/articles/brown_seely.html

Novice: *Interpret*

Teach through Social Studies

The essential question for students to consider in a study of Native Indians is, "How did the natural environment impact on the daily life and culture of aboriginal groups long ago?" Students will need to decide on an area of the country and a native nation to focus on for their investigation. Then they need to gather material from a broad range of sources. They must investigate both the physical environment of the area the native nation lived in and the cultural activities of the group. Next students need to look for relationships between physical environment and their cultural activities. This is a complex process requiring that students have some strategies to help them analyze the material they read, view and listen to.

To help students interpret data teach them how to:

- actively read, view and listen
- use features of text to focus on needed data
- read pictures, graphs, charts, diagrams and maps
- select relevant data
- make good notes
- reflect on the data gathered
- sort and classify data
- look for relationships
- make connections
- talk to others about their ideas

Gathering Evidence of Understanding

Students work with a partner to interpret a common text. Student A and B read, view, and/or listen to a section of the text. Student A distills the text to a few main points. Student B asks for clarification using a prompt. Student A responds. Students go on to another section and student B paraphrases the main ideas. Student A asks for clarification using a prompt and the process continues. Observe students as they work, noting the ability of students to interpret key messages from the text and convey them to others.

Some useful prompts

What is the meaning of...?
Do you think that...?
I think you said that...?
Why did...?
What if...? Do you agree that...?

Apprentice: *Infer*

Teach Through History

The essential question framing this study is, "How did the Industrial Revolution impact on world structures? " Students will need some good exploratory activities to give them an overview of the issues involved. Once they have explored the topic and decided on an area to investigate e.g. labor, technology, politics, economics, social issues etc., they must find reliable sources and gather their data. To discover impact of different aspects of the revolution on this time period students will need to examine events chronologically and look for cause and effect relationships. They also need to be able to make some inferences using the data they have found. To make inferences students need to apply inductive and deductive reasoning skills. Model this thinking process for students using video clips that provide concise detail about an aspect of the period e.g. the effects of urbanization, working conditions in factories etc. Work through several examples with students.

Inductive Reasoning

If:
- working conditions were unsanitary
- factory work was very dangerous
- working women also had to look after their own homes and children
- women were not paid very well

Then:
The Industrial Revolution presented many hardships for women.

Gathering Evidence of Understanding

Provide students with copies of the *Inductive Reasoning* and *Deductive Reasoning* Fig. 48-49 organizers. Instruct students to examine the data they have gathered and, using these organizers, apply their reasoning skills. Students should use the prompts on the organizers to scaffold their thinking. Have students share their inferences with others in small groups. All students should be able to articulate their findings using appropriate vocabulary to describe the steps they took in reasoning to make an inference.

InfoStar: *Predict*

Teach through Current Events

Provide students with print copies of local and national newspapers as well as access to periodical databases for back issues. Ask students to select a current issue that is in the news e.g. closing of a hospital, building of a casino, rising tuition fees etc. Instruct students to:
1) research the issue using primary and secondary sources
2) interpret the data collected
3) develop some inferences about their discoveries
4) make a prediction about the possible impact of the event
5) prepare for a town hall meeting to present their findings

Gathering Evidence of Understanding

Provide students with the organizer *Predicting Impact* Fig. 50. They should be able to record their ideas for possible effects, make a prediction, and suggest a recommendation. The organizer will provide the framework for their presentation at the Town Hall meeting where they should be express their predictions and recommendations articulately and effectively.

Notes
Reflect, Rethink, Redesign

√ Do students have a working knowledge of the prerequisite skills?
√ Have they explored the topic adequately?
√ Is the classroom atmosphere conducive to concentration and deep thinking?

Documenting the Evidence

Learner Level
Understanding of Skill
√ reads, views and listens critically to interpret text
√ makes inferences based on text, known information, and past experiences
√ utilizes prompts and organizers provided
√ applies inductive and/or deductive reasoning skills
√ makes predictions based on the reasoning processes
√ discusses with others to clarify thoughts, bounce ideas and reflect on conclusions

Notes:

Deductive Reasoning
(Fig. 48)

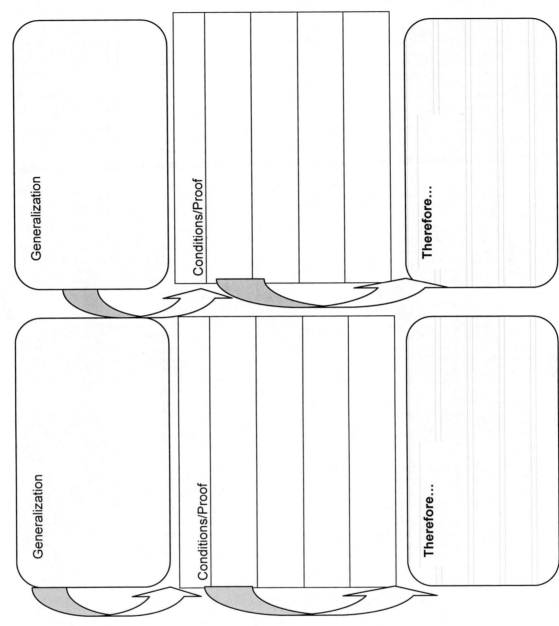

Essential Question

Generalization

Conditions/Proof

Therefore...

Generalization

Conditions/Proof

Therefore...

Examine the data you have discovered.

What are the generalizations you have discovered?

What proof have you found to substantiate the generalization?

What are the conditions that must be in place to satisfy the generalization?

What can you infer based on the generalization?

What has to be true?

Organize the data to test your deduction.

Be careful not to jump to faulty conclusions.

Make sure that you have enough quality data to base your reasoning on.

Inductive Reasoning
(Fig. 49)

Then...

If...

Essential Question:

Examine your data.

Look for patterns, connections and relationships.

What do these links tell you?

How can you explain the relationships you see?

Given the links you have discovered, what is probable?

Make some thoughtful generalizations.

Make some inferences based on your observations.

Organize the data and test out your ideas.

Do you have enough quality data to back up your reasoning?

Be careful. Don't jump to faulty conclusions!

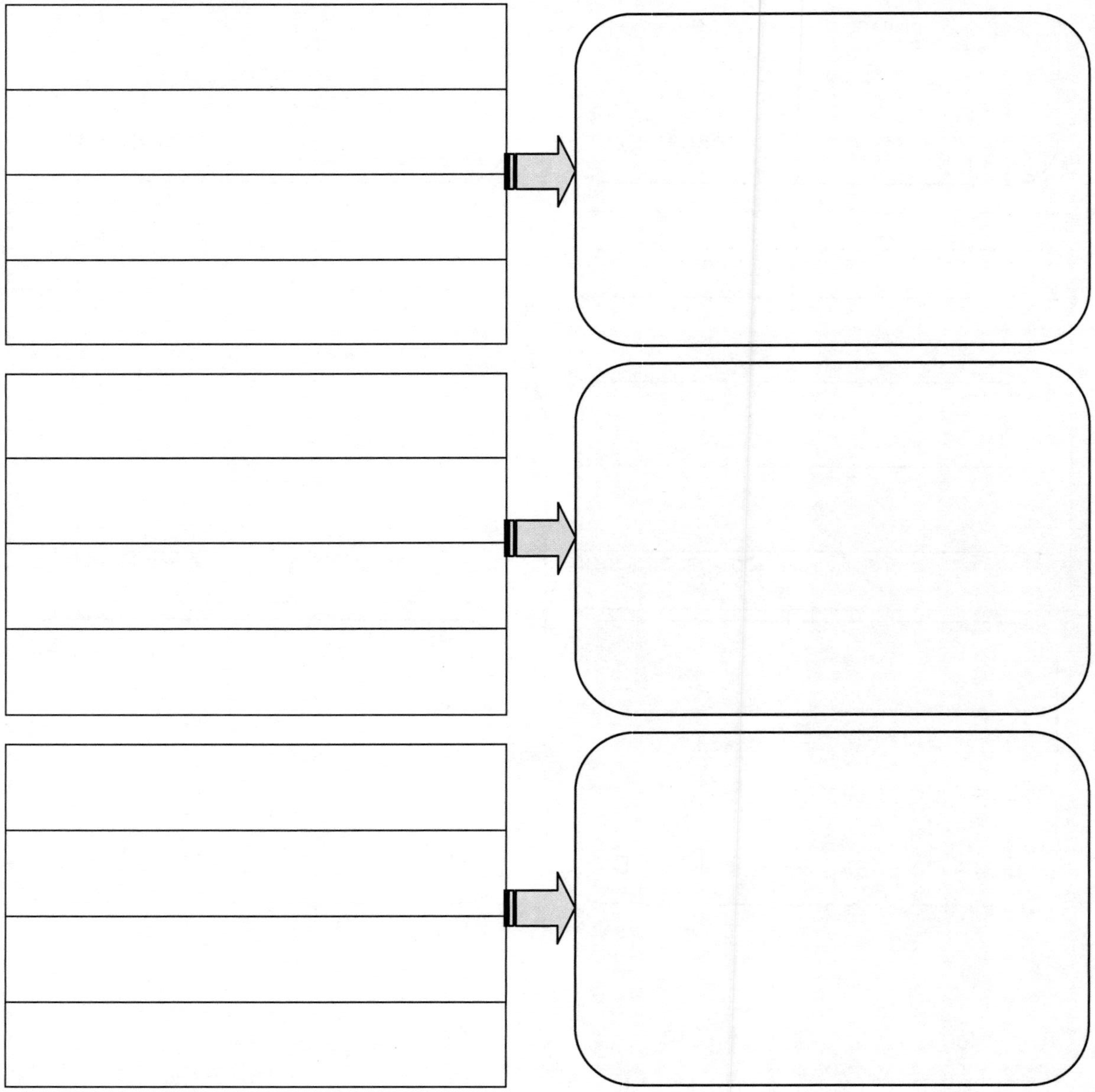

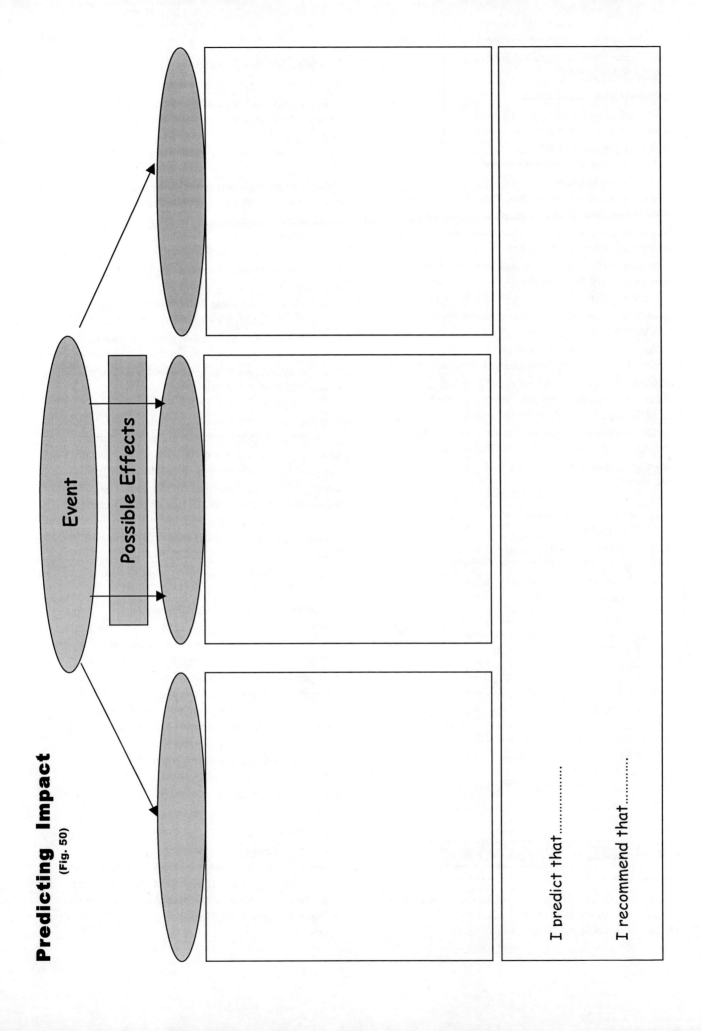

Predicting Impact

(Fig. 50)

Event

Possible Effects

I predict that............

I recommend that............

InfoSkill:

Understanding Perspective
Students will analyze information to identify and examine perspective in order to gain understanding.

Skill Discussion

Perspective is powerful when it comes to information. The ability to examine a text and determine perspective is a critical skill for working with complex issues. To be able to gain understanding through perspective requires a high level of critical thinking. Perspective, "critical and insightful points of view," is one of the six facets of understanding described by Grant Wiggins and Jay McTighe in Understanding by Design. They tell us that helping students gain perspective empowers them to be alert and put themselves a critical distance from accepted or common theories. Understanding perspective enables them to expose questionable and unexamined assumptions, conclusions and implications according to Wiggins and McTighe. This skill is useful to them as students but it is also a very important life skill.

Tips for Pondering Perspective

- What is the issue?
- What are the facts?
- Who is this issue important to? Why?
- Which factors affecting perspective do I need to consider?

❑	Gender	❑	Arts
❑	Age	❑	Environment
❑	Sex	❑	Disability
❑	Culture	❑	Country
❑	Education	❑	Occupation
❑	Politics	❑	Recreation
❑	Economics	❑	Needs

- How do these affect perspective?
- How do I know the perspective is plausible?
- How does this knowledge affect my perspective?

Link Up

• Wiggins, G., & McTighe, J. (1999). *Understanding by Design*. Alexandria VA: Association for Supervision and Curriculum Development.

Novice: *Identify Perspective*

Teach through Language

Small groups of students are reading different novels. Their task is to determine the main issue in the chapter they have just read and identify the perspective each of the main characters has about that issue.

To help students understand perspectives, give them an experience with a familiar topic e.g. a team sport such as hockey, baseball, basketball etc. Set up a scenario where Team A has just suffered a significant loss in a playoff final to Team B. Brainstorm with students all the people who would have a vested interest in the outcome of this game (The outcome being the issue.) e.g. forwards, defense, goalie, benched players, referee, linesmen, coaches, trainers, parents, friends, media, sponsors, fans, stadium owners, hospitality workers etc. Have students take on the role of different stakeholders.

Provide each student with a thought bubble and ask students to record the thoughts of that person shortly after the game ended. Share the thought bubbles and create a large chart documenting a variety of the perspectives on the game. Help students to develop a definition of perspective that is meaningful and works for them e.g. Perspective is an informed view from a special angle.

To gain perspective is to view critically and thoughtfully from all angles.

Gathering Evidence of Understanding

Provide students with the organizer *Plotting Perspective* Fig. 51 and have them individually identify the main characters and their relevant perspectives on the main issue or problem. Have students meet with others in their group (those reading the same novel) to share and discuss the perspectives they have identified. Students should be able to identify the perspective of each character and to defend their analysis with passages from the novel and/or make the necessary adjustments as they consider the ideas of their peers.

Adaptation

This skill can be introduced to pre-readers through discussion of picture books. Use cut-outs of the characters and thought bubbles to record what each character is thinking about the problem in the story, e.g. *Little Red Riding Hood, The Three Little Pigs*

N.B. *The Real Story of the Three Little Pigs by A. Wolf* by J Szeska makes a great introduction to this topic for older students.

Apprentice: *Consider Perspective*

Teach through Science and Technology

Students are preparing to investigate the impact of nuclear power plants on the quality of life in a community. They have identified the communities they plan to conduct their research on. Now they need to decide on which perspectives they need to consider in order for them to gain an accurate view of the "big picture". Provide students with time to conduct adequate exploration of the issue using video, newsreel clips, Internet sites, periodical databases etc. The purpose of this exploration is to identify all the main players on the issue (e.g. scientists, environmentalists, energy experts, economists, politicians, manufacturers, residents, employees, etc.), and their respective perspectives. List the stakeholders that students have identified for targeted research. Review *Tips for Pondering Perspective* to confirm that they have identified all relevant perspectives.

Gathering Evidence of Understanding

Have students select stakeholders whose perspective(s) they want to research and analyze in more depth. Ensure that each perspective is covered by at least one student.
Each student should be able to gather the targeted data, evaluate it, and be prepared for sharing their opinions about these perspectives during whole class discussion.

InfoStar: *Gain Insight*

Teach through Media Studies

Students are examining a national issue in order to gain insight into it. They will track the debate about the issue over a given period of time, as it is documented in news media—both print and digital/electronic—and establish a list of factual information on the issue. Each student will keep an electronic portfolio of news clips from a variety of perspectives and media types. Students will identify perspectives and analyze them utilizing *Understanding Perspectives* Fig. 52. Instruct students to look for connections between the facts they discovered and the perspectives held by specific individuals or groups. Students will document their personal reaction to each news byte in a media log.

Gathering Evidence of Understanding

Students will analyze their gathered news bytes and create a visual product to share their big picture of the issue e.g. create a graphic organizer, slide show, mini-documentary. Student should be able to identify all relevant perspectives on the issue and examine them critically to gain their own insight into the reasons for that perspective.

Sample Prompts for Media Log

- *Who is this issue important to? Why?*
- *Are their discrepancies in details reported?*
- *Do reports vary from district to district?*
- *Does the media give one perspective more weight than another? Why?*
- *Which perspectives are missing? So what?*
- *What is assumed? Is this reasonable?*
- *Why might this group/individual have this perspective?*
- *Are there any patterns or relationships in reporting? Is one theory or idea gaining momentum?*
- *Is this important? Why?*

Notes:
Reflect, Rethink, Redesign

- ◆ Did students acquire adequate background information about the issues?
- ◆ Are there still students who haven't grasped the concept that different perspectives are valid to the group that holds them?
- ◆ Is there an analogy that would help them to see the relationship?

Documenting the Evidence

Learner Level
Understanding of Skill
- ◆ articulates issue/problem
- ◆ identifies a variety of perspectives
- ◆ includes all important, relevant perspectives
- ◆ applies tips for pondering perspective
- ◆ notes factors that influence perspective
- ◆ considers reasons for specific perspectives
- ◆ *Understanding of Curriculum Content*
- ◆ sees the "big picture"
- ◆ understands that a variety of factors affect how one develops a perspective
- ◆ views issues critically and thoughtfully
- ◆ views issues dispassionately

Plotting Perspective
(Fig. 51)

Who are the main characters in the story?
What is the big issue or problem?
What is the perspective of each character
on the issue/problem?

Issue or Problem

Understanding Perspectives (Fig. 52)

Issue

Just the facts

-

-

-

-

Stakeholders

-------------------' perspective

Rationale

-------------------' perspective

Rationale

-------------------' perspective

Rationale

-------------------' perspective

Rationale

Having considered all the perspectives and the reasons for them, My perspective of this issue is ...

...because

InfoSkill:
Collaborate
Students will collaborate to enhance their understanding of information.

Skill Discussion

Collaborative learning is an instructional strategy in which students work in groups toward a common academic goal. Group work creates a powerful synergy in your classroom. Purposeful talk can enrich the processes of brainstorming, questioning, problem solving, evaluating, creating and communicating information. While working effectively in groups is a valuable skill in the world of academics, it also high on the list of employability skills and much sought after in the world of business. (Explain Fig. 53)

Before beginning group work, some management decisions must be made regarding the size of the group, roles of group members, task definition and assessment of results.

Group work is effective when students:
- brainstorm
- solve problems
- make decisions
- experiment
- research
- design, create, and construct
- work on computer tasks
- debrief a learning experience
- interpret information
- discuss a novel
- dramatize an event

Link Up

- Collaborative Learning: Group Work and Study Teams
http://teaching.berkeley.edu/bgd/collaborative.html

- Collaborative Learning
http://www.lgu.ac.uk/deliberations/collab.learning/

- Schwatz,L and Willing, K. 2001. *Computer Activities for the Cooperative Classroom* Markham, ON: Pembroke Publishers.

Novice: *Brainstorming Questions*

Teach through Geography

Students are preparing to investigate social issues resulting from migration of populations. Read and discuss a sophisticated picture book dealing with homeless people such as *Trupp* by Janell Cannon. Introduce the following collaborative strategy for interpreting text through brainstorming core questions. This strategy can be applied to getting at the essence of any issue, article, artifact, story, poem, speech, etc.

Paring to the Core

1) Think about the importance of the item presented and develop three essential questions you need answered for better understanding.
2) Share questions with a partner, discuss what you both want to discover. Cluster your thoughts to create 5 key questions about the material.
3) Form a group of four. Share everyone's questions. Discuss. Cluster ideas again and pare down to 6 essential questions.
4) Record the 6 questions on individual strips of paper or index cards. Print large!
5) Post the sets of questions from each group.
6) Sort and cluster questions. With whole group consensus pare down to 5 or 6.
7) In your group of 4 prioritize the questions and share with the large group.
8) In the large group decide on two or three core questions to frame further class and individual inquiries on the topic.

Gathering Evidence of Understanding

Provide students with a magazine or newspaper article on another related issue such as unemployment, urban sprawl or decline of the family farm. Instruct students to follow the *Paring to the Core* strategy to develop 2 or 3 essential questions on the topic. Students should demonstrate their ability to work with a partner and in small and large groups.

Adaptation

The same strategy can be used to interpret any information text (e.g. textbook, video, chart, diagram etc.) by recording key points instead of asking questions. Follow the steps to expand, cluster then pare down the points that are key to the most essential learnings.

Apprentice: *Test Ideas*

Teach through Social Studies

Students are engaged in a study of Ancient Civilizations. The Big Questions are:

• What are the enduring contributions these civilizations have made to the world?

• What are the links between today and ancient times?

Introduce to students the potential civilizations of study e.g. African, Asian, Central and South American, Ancient Mediterranean. Form teams and invite each to select an area of ancient civilization that they wish to investigate. Inform students that they will be working with their team for the duration of the process. Discuss situations where it is important to have excellent teamwork skills e.g. business world, family structures, recreation etc. Introduce the concept of assigning roles to team members. See *Team Task Prompts* Fig. 54, Assign and practice the roles of Encourager, Recorder, Worrier, and Checker. Provide teams with the scaffolding and organizers to help them access and process the information they need in to answer the big question.

Gathering Evidence of Understanding

When the project is completed have the group meet to debrief the process and particularly their group work skills. Students should complete the organizer, *Team Work Debriefing* Fig. 55 after their discussion and set goals for improvement. N.B. Ensure that, over time, students experience and practice all of the roles.

InfoStar: *Communicate Electronically*

Teach through Language

To foster independent reading set up an e-pal exchange with a school in other parts of the country or in other countries. Have students share informal comments, reflections, and questions about the books they are reading.

Set up small groups of students to network over a period of time and share their independent reading experiences.

Gathering Evidence of Understanding

Towards the end of term, instruct each small group to collaboratively create a short list of their favorite books, both fiction and non-fiction, and add brief reader's comments to each title.

They should decide on a catchy title for their list. These cross country/international favorites lists could then be shared in a number of ways with other students. Each student should contribute to the e-pal exchange throughout the year and work collaboratively in their virtual teams to develop and share the recommended lists. They might also add some titles they didn't care for and explain why those books just didn't hook their interest. (use Fig. 53)

Some e-pal Web Sites
Epals Classroom Exchange
www.epals.com
Pen Pal Class Box
www.ks-connection.org
Intercultural E-Mail Classroom Connections
www.stolaf.edu/network/iecc/
Web66
http://web66.coled.umn.edu/
Global Schoolhouse
www.gsn.org/project/index.html

Notes:
Reflect, Rethink, Redesign

♦ Which students had difficulty balancing their focus on the information task and their group role responsibilities? What can I do to help?

Documenting Evidence

Learner Level
Understanding of Skill
♦ takes responsibility for team activities
♦ values the roles of others
♦ contributes and shares ideas and information
♦ respects and listens to ideas and opinions of others
♦ listens actively
♦ encourages others to contribute
♦ perseveres to bring about consensus
♦ *Understanding Curriculum Content*
♦ experiences a broader spectrum of ideas
♦ develops greater understanding
♦ remembers more

Teaching Unit Level
See *Library Media Specialist as Agent for Collaboration* Fig. 80.

Collaboration Rubric (Fig. 53)

Achievement Level	Personal Responsibility	Support/ Appreciation	Focus	Problem Solving	Engagement
Level Four	- takes on leadership role - fulfills all aspects of the role - works as part of the team	- facilitates sharing of ideas and information - honors and praises strengths of others - assists others while respecting their roles and responsibilities	- adjusts plan as necessary to facilitate the needs of team - stays on task and reviews topic as necessary - offers positive support to help other to refocus	- is proactive in solving problems - asks probing questions and listens attentively - tests and evaluates solutions - facilitates consensus	- highly motivated - exhibits excitement - plans and works with others
Level Three	- understands personal role - fulfills assigned role duties - contributes fair share to task	- shares ideas and information - open to ideas/ point of view of others - shows awareness/ concern for feelings of others	- focuses on plan and carries it out - focuses on topic throughout task - completes all tasks on time	- uses a variety of strategies to solve problems - considers all solutions - assists others in problem solving	- very interested - positively and actively engaged - organizes task activities
Level Two	- not fully aware of role assigned - carries out some but not all role responsibilities - makes a minor contribution	- shares with reluctance - listens to ideas of others on occasion - offers some support to others	- follows plan some of the time - loses focus of topic and or plan - completes some tasks on time	- unsure how to deal with most problems - usually goes along with suggested solutions - looks to others for help	- exhibits some interest - usually cooperates with others - lacks organizational skills
Level One	- little awareness of team roles - takes no responsibility for role - contribution of little value	- little effort to share information and ideas - works in isolation - offers little support for others	- pays little attention to plan - not focused on topic or task - does not meet timelines	- gives up readily when problems arise - sometimes frustrated by problems - relies on others to solve problems	- shows no interest in activities - has difficulty working with others - is very disorganized

Team Task Prompts (Fig. 54)

Today you are the **Encourager**

- ❏ Is the group on track?
- ❏ Use positive body, language thumbs up, nod, smile.
- ❏ Use positive language - good job, that's it, great idea, let's go for it,
- ❏ just a little more to do, you are a great team, keep thinking

Today you are the **Recorder**

- ❏ Record all ideas.
- ❏ Don't comment or make judgments, just record.
- ❏ Use abbreviations and symbols to keep up.
- ❏ Ask for clarification if you are unsure of what was said.
- ❏ Paraphrase when necessary and confirm your interpretation of ideas presented.

Today you are the **Worrier**

- ❏ Does the team agree on the task?
- ❏ Is the team keeping on task?
- ❏ Is everyone contributing?
- ❏ When is the task due?
- ❏ How much time is left?
- ❏ Is everyone being considerate?
- ❏ Are we working as a team?
- ❏ Did we forget anything?

Today you are the **Checker**

- ❏ Does everyone understand his/her job?
- ❏ Does everyone understand the task?
- ❏ Do we have all the materials/resources we need?
- ❏ Have we checked the evaluation criteria?
- ❏ Have we completed our task?

Team Work Debriefing (Fig. 55)

Everyone on the team had an important job to do.
How well did we do our jobs?

Team spirit

Team effort

Meeting task expectations

Meeting timelines

Quality of our work

Goals for next time

Working as a group helped us to...

Part 5: Synthesize

After students have analyzed their information, broken it down and looked at it in different ways, they are ready to do something new with it. It is of supreme importance that students invest time in meaningful analysis before attempting to synthesize. Without this investment their results in synthesis stage will be at best "thinsesis."

Now the students are ready. How do we proceed? What do we want to happen for students?
In the synthesis stage students begin to experience the "aha's" of learning. They discover how their new learning can work for them. They often experience a surge of creativity, a desire to do something with what they have learned.

The *Synthesis* stage is totally dependent on the foregoing stages of the research process and is blended with *Share and Use* and *Reflect, Transfer and Apply* stages. The form that the synthesis takes on is closely linked to the topic and the focus of the foregoing study.
e.g. A student who has investigated the mechanics of a bicycle braking system will discover why his brakes are malfunctioning and be able to repair them or write up a procedure for others to do the repair.

The students who investigated how design and materials impact on reliability, weight and speed of a bicycle may create new designs for racing bikes.
When students have studied the variety of perspectives surrounding a controversial issue such teenagers and fast food, and understand the various concerns, they are able to make recommendations for workable solutions. The synthesis for study of healthy eating for young adults may result in a series of videotaped cooking shows for college students living away from home for the first time.

The variety of synthesis activities is limited only by imagination. Considering this we have taken a different approach to the last three sections of *Build Your Own: Information Literate School.*
We have provided tools to help develop skills. These tools can be adapted and applied to a wide variety of situations and scenarios. Reflect on the targeted learning and select the tools that best match your goals. Model their use and gradually guide your students towards independence.

(p146) Synthesize
      Novice: Model Conferencing to Synthesize
      Apprentice: Use Organizers to Synthesize
      InfoStar: Design Synthesis Organizers and Thinking Process Maps

(Fig.56) Synthesis Chart
      Select thinking stems appropriate to your goals and apply them to prompt synthesis.

(Fig.57) Perspective, Argument, Thesis

(Fig.58) Solve a Problem, Construct a New Hypothesis

(Fig.59) Consider Alternative Ideas; Make a Judgment or Predition

(Fig.60) Draw Conclusions

(Fig.61) Develop Generalizations

(Fig.62) Make a Decision

InfoSkill:

Synthesize
Students will synthesize information to answer their inquiry question and/or create something new.

Skill Discussion

In the foregoing section we focused on **Analysis**, the close inspection of the collected data and the ideas of others. Analysis involves taking information apart and working with it by regrouping and reorganizing it to look for new and original patterns.

To analyze, students:
• sort and compare or classify
• look for patterns and trends
• find relationships or connections
• determine cause and effect
• identify and predict impact
• interpret, infer, predict
• identify perspectives

Only after careful analysis, can students begin productive **synthesis.** When they synthesize students take all the parts identified and put them back together again in a new meaningful way. Through synthesis students build understanding and create new personal knowledge.

When students synthesize they:
• Develop generalizations and report.
• Consider alternatives and make a judgment or prediction.
• Draw conclusions.
• Make decisions.
• Gain perspective and develop an argument or a thesis.
• Explore solutions and solve a problem or construct a new hypothesis.

Having done this, students will be ready to plan how to share their new knowledge so that others can learn from them. As they are creating their product or presentation, students are constructing personal knowledge. At this time students write, create, invent, compose, plan, imagine... Although this is all part of synthesis, we will deal with actually communicating learning in the following section entitled *Share and Use* p. 155.

All of the skills and tasks we have developed in foregoing sections of this book lead up to the synthesis stage of the research process. Without the previous stages meaningful synthesis cannot take place. The inquiry question and nature of the content along with individual student experiences and connections are the catalysts for synthesis. Rather than develop specific tasks at this stage we will share some generic strategies for you to try with your students. Please don't abandon them at this point in the process. They need your guidance and facilitation even more now that they have found all this great information. This InfoSkill will provide some strategies to help students synthesize and gain personal knowledge.

Novice: *Model Conferencing to Synthesize*

After gathering and analyzing a body of information on a particular curriculum inquiry, plan to model the synthesis stage. Review the inquiry question or statement of purpose. Decide the form of the synthesis based on the question, the nature of the content, student experience.... Select the appropriate question stems from the *Synthesis Chart* Fig. 56 to model a "think aloud" conference with the class. Through purposeful talk students will make generalizations, draw conclusions, develop a perspective, consider alternatives, or solve problems etc. Use a curriculum topic or an item of current interest to the students. e.g.
- What are the major consequences of making the school cafeteria menu nutrition conscious?
- Why are the cod fishing stocks declining? Use lots and lots of talk to model for students the thought processes that take place when synthesizing and making new discoveries. Record the new ideas. Guide students as they work together to develop generalizations, conclusions, decisions, perspectives, or solutions etc. It is critical that students understand how these steps impact on the success of their final product. Model how to take the new ideas and turn them into a product or presentation such as a report, letter to the editor, poem, dramatic skit, advertisement, web page, etc. See *Share and Use* p. 155.

Gathering Evidence of Understanding

On the next research task have students conference in small groups test out ideas with the support of a peer. Students should review their inquiry question or information task, then select the appropriate question stems from the *Synthesis Chart* to help them frame their discussions. They will require lots of practice with each kind of synthesis.

Adaptation

Young researchers can learn to draw conclusions and summarize their findings if we give them appropriate stems to facilitate their thinking. e.g.

> The big idea I have discovered is....
> I think that.....
> I have discovered that.....
> This is important because.....
> I wonder if........
> I believe that......
> Perhaps.....
> I wondered about ... I discovered ...

Apprentice: *Use Organizers to Synthesize*

Specifically designed graphic organizers that guide students to critical thinking will help them to construct new meaning. Graphic organizers are effective tools to give students a "mind's-eye" view of information processing. Providing structure guides original thought. Since the synthesis process is very complex and abstract, anything we can do to make it more concrete for students will help build personal understanding. We have developed several graphic organizers to prompt synthesis. Use them or adapt them for specific topics. See *Developing Generali-zations, Drawing Conclusions, Gaining Perspective, Considering Alternatives* and *Exploring Solutions Fig. 57-62.* Model the usage of each of the synthesis graphic organizers provided in this section. Give students opportunities to practice using each of these tools and later to create their own variations and combinations to suit specific information tasks.

Gathering Evidence of Understanding

Since most of the process at this point becomes thinking "inloud" we need to ask students to articulate how the organizing tool helped them to put their thoughts and ideas together. They should be able to describe how the spaces, prompts, arrows and flow of a graphic organizer help them to build personal understanding and spark creative thought.

Adaptation

Synthesis organizers are excellent pre-writing tools. Students can use them to prepare for writing a report, editorial, argumentative essay, press release etc.

InfoStar:: *Design Synthesis Organizers and Thinking Process Maps*

As discussed in the InfoSkill *Use Organizers* p. 90. The aim is for students to develop their own visual tools to help them think through a complex information problem. Another excellent synthesis tool is a thinking process map. It really is a "think it out" while formally doodling prior knowledge, new ideas, connections and questions. While students construct their thinking process maps they are literally building their own understanding. Several commercial software tools are available to support this skill. Model their use and provide lots of practice. Students should progress through stages from working with these strategies in teacher-guided sessions, with teacher created tools, to adapting and then eventually developing their own.

Gathering Evidence of Understanding

Students create a graphic organizer or a visual map of their thinking to provide a real snapshot of achievement. This offers teachers an opportunity to really "see" what the student has accomplished. Students should demonstrate:
- detailed knowledge of content
- broad content concepts
- links and relationships within content and to prior learning
- cross discipline and curricular connections
- evidence of perspective
- creative thought and imagination
- problem-solving and decision making

Link Up
- Hyerle, David. 1996. *Visual Tools for Constructing Knowledge* Alexandria, Virginia : ASCD Concept Maps http://classes.aces.uiuc.edu/ACES100/Mind/CMap.html

- The Concept Mapping Homepage http://users.edte.utwente.nl/lanzing/cm_home.htm

- Off Road Thinking: Looking for Great Surprise http://optin.iserver.net/fromnow/jan02/surprise.html

Synthesis Chart
(Fig. 56)

Combining Ideas to Make a New Whole	Synthesis Thinking Stems
Develop generalizations and report importance.	• What are the big ideas you have discovered? • What are the supporting details? • Which are facts? Which are opinions? • What seems important? • How does.....relate to.....? • Some examples are..... • How does...impact on....? • What does the impact mean for stakeholders?
Draw conclusions.	• The main issue is..... • If this is true then.... • How do you feel about it? • What did you learn about....? • Why is this new knowledge important? • Are there conflicting viewpoints? • What are the pros and cons? • What is "iffy"? • Is some information missing? • What questions do you still have? • What if...?
Make decisions.	• What has to be decided? • What are the conditions, restrictions, limitations, obstacles? • My ideas for possible solutions are... • What are the pros and cons of my solution suggestions? • The two best ideas are... • A combination of ... idea and ... ideas might work because... • My best solution suggestion is...
Gain perspective and develop an argument or thesis.	• What are the facts? • What are the opinions of others? • What are the alternatives? • In view of this, I think... • The evidence suggests... • Contributing factors ... • What is your point of view?
Consider alternatives and make a judgment or prediction.	• What might happen if...? • What would be a better idea? • What do you predict...? • Suppose......
Explore solutions and solve a problem or construct a new hypothesis.	• What is the problem? • Why is it a problem? • Who is it a problem for? • What data are available? current, past • What is predicted? By whom? • Can you make a chart or diagram to illustrate the problem? • What are the causes and their effects? • What are your thoughts about it? • What solutions do you suggest? • How could this dilemma be solved?

Synthesis (Fig. 57)

Use this organizer to help you gain **perspective** and develop an **argument/thesis**.

Inquiry question

.........................."s Perspective

.........................."s Perspective

Reason:

.........................."s Perspective

.........................."s Perspective

Reason:

Reason:

Reason:

Similarities

Differences

My argument/thesis statement

Synthesis (Fig. 58)

Use this organizer to explore solutions and solve a **problem** or construct a new **hypothesis**.

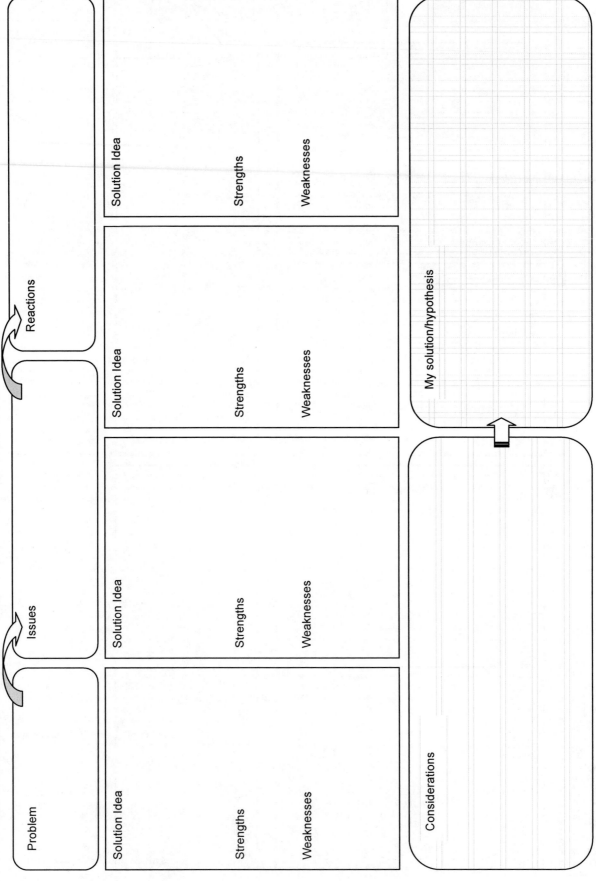

Problem

Issues

Reactions

Solution Idea

Strengths

Weaknesses

Solution Idea

Strengths

Weaknesses

Solution Idea

Strengths

Weaknesses

Solution Idea

Strengths

Weaknesses

My solution/hypothesis

Considerations

Synthesize (Fig. 59)

Use this organizer to consider alternative ideas and make a **judgement** or prediction.

Issue

What might happen if.......?

So What!

What is really important is....

+ -

Evaluation of alternatives

Judgment/Prediction

Synthesis (Fig. 60)

Inquiry Question/Problem

Use this organizer to draw **conclusions**.

My Ideas	Supporting Data

Have I examined all relevant points of view? Can I identify patterns and trends? Based on this evidence, what conclusions can I draw?

How can I use my new knowledge? What do I believe is important? Why? How can I share it with others?

Adapted from *InfoTasks for Successful Learning*, Pembroke Publishers 2001.

Synthesis (Fig. 61)

Use this organizer to develop **generalizations**.

Inquiry Question

Important Points

Supporting facts & ideas

Supporting facts & ideas

Supporting facts & ideas

Supporting facts & ideas

Supporting facts & ideas

Supporting facts & ideas

Look for connections, relationships and discrepancies.   **Answer your inquiry question.**

Generalization

My Thoughts

Synthesis (Fig. 62)

Use this organizer to help you make a **decision**.

My problem is _____

so I need to decide _____

Limitations, obstacles, conditions etc.
Solution Criteria, "must haves"

Great Ideas	Pro/Cons

Select your two better solution ideas.
Which one best meets your solution criteria?

I have decided

Because…

Part 6: Share and Use

Students are now ready to communicate and demonstrate what they have learned. This is the tangible part of synthesis and a true test of their understanding. Wiggins and McTighe tell us " You understand it only if you can teach it, use it, prove it, explain it, defend it or read between the lines."

Student will require lots of modeling and guidance with a variety of presentation formats until they become skilled enough to independently select the format and create the presentation on their own.
There is a huge potential here for creativity as well as a great opportunity to appeal to, and benefit from, different intelligences. Students may apply their new learning to solve a hands-on problem or create something new. This is a chance for us as educators to make curriculum more relevant for students. Realistic roles and presentation scenarios make it is easier for students to see the connections between life and learning.

The presentation they create could be oral, visual, written or multimedia. In this section of *Build Your Own: Information Literate School* we have provided some guidance and tools to help develop the skills students will need to be able to effectively share and use their new knowledge.

(p156) Share and Use
Novice: Teacher Selected and Modeled Products and Presentations
Apprentice: Teacher Guided Products and Presentations
InfoStar: Student Choice and Design

(Fig. 63) Planning for Sharing Rubric
Explain and discuss this rubric up front in the planning stage so students know how this part of the process will be evaluated and can use the breakdown in the different sections and levels to help them meet their personal goals.

(Fig. 64) Presentation Rubric
Explain and discuss this rubric early in the process so students know how the presentation will be evaluated and can use the breakdown in the different sections and levels to help them meet their personal goals.

(Fig. 65) Real World Roles (Based on *Six Facets of Learning*, Wiggins and McTighe 1999)
Real World Roles is a collection of ideas to help you integrate the Six Facets of Learning into the students' demonstration of their new learning. This chart suggests exciting "real world" roles for students to take on as they create and present their demonstrations. Consider the subject and content as you, and ultimately your students, select roles and demonstrations that realistically enhance the content.

(Fig. 66) Planning for Writing Information Text
This chart provides a comprehensive blending of specific written formats with appropriate organizers to help students visualize their plan and see the flow of their writing, as well as focus words and tips to guide them through the process.

(Fig. 67-68) Plans for Sharing Your Research
Students need to consider a number of variables as they select a "do-able" format for their presentations. Part 1 of this organizer guides the students through the necessary steps in the process of choosing a presentation format. Part 2 provides a checklist to ensure that they develop their plans effectively and reflect on the presentation to plan for improvement.

InfoSkill:

Share and Use
Students will share and use their new knowledge and insight.

Skill Discussion

This is the stage in the inquiry process where students can strut their stuff and show you and their peers all what they have accomplished. Again, this stage requires lots of carefully planned teaching and guidance. Ultimately we want students to select the format, create, and present independently. In preparation for this independence, we need to teach the process of creating a variety of presentations Fig. 64. At first students will require many experiences where the product/ presentation is teacher-selected and guided. They will build strategies from which to select and to apply as needed. As they accumulate these experiences we need to define the steps involved and establish criteria for evaluation so that students have a understanding of what is expected. Students need guidance so that they can match their content to the best format for delivering their message. They need to be exposed to lots of excellent formats so they know what a good book, magazine article, video, skit, pamphlet, or web site looks like and sounds like. Teach students how to write non-fiction. Their work doesn't have to sound like an encyclopedia article (Harvey 1998). Be careful to balance the marking, honoring all stages of the research process. Often students put so much emphasis on the product/presentation that process and new knowledge are lost in glitzy appearance and pizzazz. We can counteract this by clearly including specifics regarding content and process skills in the evaluation outline that we share with students before they begin.

There are several major components to this large information skill.

Students need to:
• Decide on the best format.
• Develop a plan.
• Utilize appropriate technologies.
• Cite all information sources.
• Test ideas and practice.
• Communicate new learning

Time spent building these skills at the Novice and Apprentice stages will pay huge dividends later. See *Real World Roles* Fig. 65 to help you design effective and engaging tasks that help students build deeper understanding of their research topic.

Novice: *Teacher Selected and Modeled Products/Presentations*

Guide students through the creation of a variety of presentation formats designed to model all the components of this stage of research. Make links between the content, the intended audience, and the format selected. Give them practice sharing in a variety of ways: written, oral, visual, and combinations including multimedia.

1) Select and model a format that compliments the new knowledge students have.
  • Community helpers - dramatization
  • Life cycle of butterflies - labeled circle chart
  • Seasonal change - write a chant
  • Animal habitats - class big book
  • An excursion - letter to parents
  • Aquatic animals - design a mural
  • Caring for a pet - create a slideshow
  • Environmental sound - soundscape, multimedia

2) Develop a plan with students and put it on chart paper.
  • How will we share our new learning?
  • Who will our audience be?
  • What materials and equipment do we need?
  • How will we use our new knowledge?
  • What all do we need to do?
  • Who will do each job?
  • How much time do we have?
  • When do we need to finish certain things in order to be ready on time?
  • When and where will we practice?
  • Who will give us feedback for revision?
  • When and where will we present?
  • How will we know we have done a good job?
Check off as each task as it is completed.

3) Model making use of appropriate technologies to prepare and share the class product/presentation.
  • Videotape a play or report and view it to critique and make improvements.
  • Record a song on tape for sharing with other classes and parents.
  • Word process a report or letter and copy for distribution.
  • Take digital photographs during an excursion and print to use in a class report or on the school Web Page.
  • Send a class poem to e-pals.
  • Hold a press conference.

4) Before going live with sharing give students enough time and space to practice. Guide them to revisit the task description and evaluation outline, reflect on how they have done, and if necessary rethink and rework.

5) Set up a time, place, and an authentic audience for students to present their collaborative sharing and then celebrate your successes.

Gathering Evidence of Success

Have students record the process of preparing and sharing in their journals using procedure writing. Students should be able to document each step taken by the class.

Apprentice: *Guided Planning and Writing of Information Text*

Teach the basic organizational structures for information text. See *Planning for Writing Information Text* Fig. 66. Model for students how visual organizers can help plan for writing. Provide students with exemplars for different kinds of information texts. e.g. pamphlet, press release, letter to the editor, editorial, magazine article, manual. Ask students to sort and categorize them by organizational structure. Have students examine the exemplars and decide which format or combination of formats would best help them share their new knowledge and insight.

Gathering Evidence of Understanding

Students will decide on an information text format that best matches their sharing needs. They will select a visual organizer and use it to map out the gathered information ready to write their first draft. Before they begin to work on their first draft they should conference with a teacher. Students should be able to use a visual organizer to plan for writing and compliment their presentation with visual information text such as charts, maps, diagrams, graphs and sketches. Provide students with clear guidelines as to assessment criteria, timelines, and audience at the beginning of the project.

InfoStar: *Student Choice and Plan*

Brainstorm with students formats that would be good for sharing their new knowledge with others. Put each idea on a card or large sticky note and post so everyone can see the growing list. Prepare three overlapping circles on the chalkboard to create a triple Venn or place three hula-hoops overlapping on the floor. Label each circle **oral**, **visual** and **written**. Have students sort the

presentation formats and place them in the appropriate section of the triple Venn *(Koechlin and Zwaan)*. Instruct students to refer to the triple Venn to consider formats for presenting their research findings. Encourage students to take advantage of their special talents and skills but also to work on developing new talents e.g. utilizing technologies and integrating the arts. Provide students with an organizer with prompts to help them plan and prepare for their presentation. See *Plans for Sharing Your Research* Fig. 67-68. Remind students to consider:

* interests, age and background knowledge of their intended audience
* personal skills and talents
* time constraints
* availability of equipment

Gathering Evidence of Understanding

Provide students with a rubric or marking scale and discuss how their product/ presentation will be graded. See *Planning for Sharing Rubric* Fig. 63 and *Presentation Rubric* Fig. 64.

Adaptation

Work with students to identify the criteria that could be used to assess a product/ presentation e.g. format, information shared, organization, originality, audience response, etc. Have students work in groups to develop rubrics or check lists to evaluate their achievement in the presentation of their new knowledge. Share assessment criteria developed by groups and decide on the assessment tool that will be used by the class. Students should develop a presentation, in the format of their choice, which meets the predetermined criteria. They should use the class assessment tool to self-evaluate.

Link Up

* Harvey, Stephanie. 1998. *Non-Fiction Matters*, York, Maine: Stenhouse Publishers.

* Fletcher, R. and Portalupi, J. 2001. *Non-Fiction Craft Lessons: Teaching Information Writing K-8*. York, Maine: Stenhouse Publishers.

* Koechlin, C., & Zwaan, S. (1997). *Information Power Pack: Intermediate*. Markham, ON: Pembroke.

Planning for Sharing Rubric (Fig. 63)

Achievement Level	Understands Task	Collects and Analyzes Data	Time Management	Selects Format for Sharing	Plans Presentation
Level Four	- understands task requirements and is able explain so others understand - understands evaluation tools and is able to clarify these for others	- devises note making techniques - creates organizers - all information collected relates directly to topic and includes relevant data to enhance topic	- creates a planning tool to organize work - meets all deadlines and allows time to deal with unexpected glitches	- combines formats or creates an original appropriate for audience - understands and can explain format criteria - understands format needs and considers all factors (personal skills, talents, needs, support, timelines) independently	- meticulous planning includes contingency arrangements for unexpected equipment breakdowns and other glitches - practices or previews for others and makes necessary changes, rehearses again - prearranges and tests setup
Level Three	- articulates requirements clearly and completely - understands marking scheme/evaluation tools	- uses note making techniques - selects and uses appropriate organizers - data collected relates to the topic - data supports needs for end product	- uses a planning tool to realistically chunk work - meets all deadlines	- considers formats, selects one appropriate for audience - understands format criteria - considers list of factors to select format - decides on format based on above criteria	- plans carefully, arranges for materials and equipment required - rehearses, practices makes some adjustments - prearranges set up
Level Two	- articulation reveals some confusion about task requirements - is aware of marking scheme/evaluation tools	- little evidence note making techniques - needs assistance to select an organizer - data collections lack organization - some data unsuitable	- little evidence of advanced planning - meets some deadlines	- considers formats but makes inappropriate selection - somewhat confused about format criteria - finds list of factors to guide selection confusing	- incomplete planning, scrambles for materials and or equipment at last minute - practices, makes no changes - does last minute setup
Level One	- unable to articulate what is expected - disregards implications of marking scheme/evaluation tools	- no evidence of use of note making techniques - no evidence of use of organizers - data collected not useable for final product - too much or too little data	- no evidence of advanced planning - doesn't recognize and or adhere to timelines, requires reminders	- randomly selects format for sharing - no evidence of understanding of criteria - little or no evidence of understanding of factors to guide format selection	- little evidence of organized and thoughtful planning - no evidence of practice - set up not preplanned

Presentation Rubric (Fig. 64)

Achievement Level	Information	Organization	Audience Consideration	Citation	Knowledge
Level Four	- information rich - subject effectively enhanced - outstanding introduction - excellent summary	- imaginative arrangement of subtopics - creative use of supporting data	- adjusted to background knowledge and reactions of audience - uses creative techniques to capture audience - enthusiastic audience response	- all sources identified and cited accurately and additional information sources provided	- answers questions and elaborates on the topic
Level Three	- all data accurate and on topic - topic well introduced - accurately summarized	- logical organization of appropriate subtopics - includes supporting data	- well attuned to audience interests - exhibits originality - maintains audience interest	- all sources identified and cited accurately	- answers questions accurately and confidently
Level Two	- most information on topic and correct - weak introduction - poor summary	- some evidence of subtopics - some supporting data	- some evidence of planning to take into account the knowledge and interest of the audience -lacks originality - audience was partially, somewhat interested	- identified some sources	- answers some questions accurately
Level One	- too much/little information - some information off topic or incorrect - little attention paid to either introduction or summary	- no evidence of subtopics - supporting data not sorted	- too complicated or too simple for audience - no creative elements - didn't keep audience attention	- no source information for data	- unable to provide answers to topic related questions of peers and teacher

Real World Roles (Fig. 65)

Based on the Six Facets of Learning

Facet	Role	Demonstration of Understanding
(Wiggins & McTighe 1999)		
Explanation Sophisticated and apt explanations and theories, which provide knowledgeable and justified accounts of events, actions, and ideas.	newscaster, weather forecaster, reporter, journalist scriptwriter, teacher, instructor photographer, author, cartographer, illustrator, biographer city planner, designer, writer, advertiser, graphic artist, layout artist politician, press officer, representative	- forecast, predict, environmental scan, videoconference, report of interview, log, - cooking show segments, infomercial, docudrama, travelogue show, internet website page, - photographic story, written story, map (e.g. school neighborhood), - create a bulletin board, model, profile visual or written, displays community plan visual or written (e.g. traffic flow, transit, green areas.) - advertisements, manuals, catalogue descriptions (e.g. describe gallery artifacts, clothing, furniture), press release - scrum, press conference, delegation, sales representative
Interpretation Interpretations, narratives, and translations that provide meaning.	columnist, television show host/guest, literary critic, judge, lawyer, translator, interpreter, newscaster, photographer, author, artist, illustrator, poet, cartoonist, filmmaker	- review e.g. book, movie, play, concert, tour, travel destination - trial, contest, broadcast - magazine article, pamphlet, news broadcast, advertisement - photo journal, picture book, story, cartoon - web, mind map
Application The ability to use knowledge effectively in new situations.	travel consultant, city planner, taxi driver technician, mechanic, detective, firefighter designer, inventor, architect, gardener composer, woodworker, carpenter, builder, caterer, chef actor, singer, speaker, sports pro,	- plan a route, vacation plan, city plans e.g. parks transportation, plaza etc - use a new skill to solve a problem, make a repair, fight a fire - create games, create a butterfly garden, write a song - build a bat house, skateboard ramp, create a balanced menu - perform music, speech, role, gymnastics, athletics...
Perspective Critical and insightful point of view.	analyst, pollster, marketing researcher lobbyist, debater, panelist, candidate	- impact study - effect of cell phones on..., effect of video games on... - effect of personal mini CD burners on artists, vendors, producers - town hall meeting, T.V. show, debate, candidates meeting, press conference
Empathy The ability to identify with another person's feelings and worldview.	talk show host, press secretary, interviewer, journalist, columnist, activist, lawyer	- participate in a talk show, promotion, press conference, study group, commission, summit, forum, investigation, simulation, road show, - interview in role,
Self Knowledge The wisdom to know one's ignorance and how one's patterns of thought and action inform as well as prejudice understanding.	self assessor, reflective thinker and learner, future planner	- write a position paper, learning log, journal, exposition, express an opinion, argument, personal perspective, - reflect on performance, self evaluate, - set goals, recognize importance of learning

Planning for Writing Information Text (Fig.66)

These are some common structures used for writing information text. Think about your research quest and the data you have gathered. What structure or combination of structures would work well for sharing your findings? Use a graphic organizer to help you plan for writing. The focus words and tips will help if you get stuck putting your thoughts together.

Organizational Structure	Visual aid for planning	Focus words and tips
Question and Answer -ask a question and answer it	T Chart	Who, what, when, where, why, how **Plan your order carefully.**
Sequence -putting facts, events in an order	Timeline to arrange events chronologically Storyboard to plan change over time	On…,not long after, now, before, after, when, first, second, then, finally, during, next, **Check for accuracy**
Comparison -pointing out similarities and differences	Venn diagram Triple T Chart	Similarly, however, but, on the other hand, compared to, despite, as opposed to, nevertheless **Establish criteria for comparison**
Cause and Effect -Show a causal relationship. -Demonstrate what led to a certain effect	Flow Chart to illustrate links Fishbone diagram to cluster causes	Because, since, therefore, consequently, since, so, accordingly, as a result, on account of, due to. Then **Investigate all relevant perspectives**
Problem Solution -state a problem and offer several solutions	Flow chart Web Diagram	A solution, consider, possibly, perhaps, since, this led to, **Test your solution ideas with a friend**
Procedure -list step by step	Storyboard to show change over time Flow chart to show process	First, next, following that, finally **Add visual aids**
Report or description -provide structure to a reworking of collected data	Web to brainstorm and organize Table to sort topic into subtopics Tree diagram to sort a topic into groups and sub-groups Sketch ,map or diagram to organize detail	Use your own language and writing style. Use quotation marks for direct quotes from the work of others. Use citations to indicate the ideas of others you have used in your report. **Be accurate**
Argument -project a personal point of view	Web to brainstorm ideas Table to compare opposing points of view Chart to analyze pros and cons Flow chart to organize and link reasoning	Begin with a strong statement or question. Support your opinion with facts and evidence **End firmly**

Planning Notes

Plans for Sharing Your Research - Part 1 (Fig. 67)

Why? Your inquiry question

What? Your new knowledge or big idea

Who? Audience

How? Assessment criteria

When? Date/Time

Where? Location

What presentation format is best? Record your ideas in the boxes below. List a variety of possible formats that would be effective for this topic. Think about your own strengths and weaknesses. State the pluses and minuses of each format you are interested in. Evaluate your choices. Narrow it down to three and discuss your choices with a friend, parent and/or a teacher.
Then decide which format is best.

Format - oral, visual, written, multimedia	Positive	Negative	Best three choices
Your decision			

Plans for Sharing Research - Part 2 (Fig. 68)

❏ You have decided on a format.

❏ Now you need to plan how to organize your information. Use a visual organizer to help you prepare for writing or creating.

❏ Write, sketch, or create a first draft/plan.

❏ Conference with a friend and make revisions if necessary.

❏ Prepare the final version of your presentation.

❏ Rehearse. (with a friend, in front of a mirror, using a tape recorder, using a video camera)

❏ Time your presentation.

❏ Make revisions as necessary.

❏ Check and double check that you have everything you need.

❏ Be prepared to answer questions from your audience.

❏ Get a good rest the night before your presentation.

❏ Be confident you have something special to share!

How did you do?

What went well?

What were the glitches?

Is there something you'd like to improve on? Why and how?

Overall, how do you feel about it?

Notes:

Part 7: Reflect Transfer and Apply

Students have completed their research quest. They have experienced the angst of grappling with a new assignment, the excitement of discovery, and the elation of sharing. Now is the time for them to stand back and reflect on their learning. They need to consider their effort as well as their progress. We also need to provide opportunity for students to take their research to another level if they are motivated to do so. The application and transference of their learning to new situations is the ultimate learning experience.

We want students to take personal responsibility for their learning. In order to develop the reflecting and questioning skills needed to do this, students will require many tools and lots of practice. There are prompts, checklists, and rubrics provided throughout *Build Your Own: Information Literate School* to assist your students as they become personally responsible. The *Documenting Evidence* section of each *InfoSkills* contains criteria you can use to create additional checklists and rubrics to guide student self-assessment. We have included some additional tools in this section to help students think about what they have achieved, their personal effort, and what they need to do to improve.

(p166) Reflect Transfer and Apply
   Novice: Reflect and Self-Evaluate
   Apprentice: Set and Reach for Goals
   InfoStar: Apply New Learning and Take Action

(Fig.69-70) Research Success Rubric
   This is a very detailed rubric for assessing the major components of the research process. Cut and paste sections of it so you can evaluate the skills you are focusing on at any given time or use it to evaluate the entire process.

(Fig.71) Assessing My Effort
   Students can complete this organizer in preparation for a conference with the teacher or library media specialist. This exercise will help students to associate effort with results.

(Fig.72) My Research Reflections
   Use this organizer as an overview to help students assess their achievement in general and make some plans for improvement on the next project. Discuss the importance and value of honest self-evaluation and encourage students to make realistic suggestions for improvement. Have students review these before and after their next project to check their progress.

(Fig.73) Planning for Improvement
   Communication is key to effective assessment. Parents want and need to be involved as they often provide the guidance and support for larger projects on the homefront. This organizer is a great vehicle for focusing and aligning aspirations and activities for students, parent and teachers.

InfoSkill:

Reflect, Transfer and Apply
Students will reflect on their work, and transfer and apply their learning to new situations.

Skill Discussion

This stage of the research process marks the end of the immediate information task and sets the stage for further investigations or applications of the new learning. Students must have metacognitive experiences all through the process as well as at the completion of their sharing in order for real learning to occur. Always provide students with clear indicators of success (e.g. rubrics and checklists) before research begins. This guidance should help students to:

• reflect on the process and the product.
• self-evaluate their effort and their accomplishments.
• set goals for both short term and long term improvement.
• apply their new learning to other experiences and disciplines.
• take informed action based on their research, discoveries, and conclusions.

Provide students with examples of transfer in areas they are already familiar with. Collect examples of great picture books that are based on factual information.

- Examine historical and science fiction novels and discuss the research that forms the backbone. Ask students to explain why this research is necessary.
- Discuss other activities that require transfer of knowledge and/or skills from one discipline to another.
- Provide students with information about organizations and actions where youth are involved and must apply their knowledge and take action.

Link Up

• Keilburger, Craig and Marc. *Take Action: A Guide to Active Citizenship.*

• Leaders Today
www.leaderstoday.com
• Kids Can Free the Children
www.freethechildren.org/peace/mainindex.html
 • World Wildlife Fund
www.panda.org
• International Red Cross
www.icrc.org/

Novice: *Reflect and Self-evaluate*

Introduce the concept of reflection with a picture book and or novels where the protagonist thinks back in time and reflects on events or accomplishments in the past. Record the dialogue in thought bubbles. Hold a sharing circle asking students to think about and share something they are proud of, something that made them feel very happy or sad etc.

At first they will need to be guided through the process with lots of modeling, talk aloud, and prompts. Eventually, after much practice, it will become a natural component of how students approach learning.

Gathering Evidence of Understanding

When students self-evaluate and think about their learning, they should be able to discuss their actual progress or performance, their personal effort, and how they feel about what they are learning and doing. There are many tools to help student actively think about their learning throughout the research process.

Some strategies to try:

• conference both with teacher and peers
• discuss with a caregiver
• research portfolios with a learning log
• research journals
• sticky notes
• thought bubbles
• study groups to talk about and test ideas
• rubrics with clear criteria and achievable indicators
• assessment checklist - self, peer and teacher
• exemplars of best practice
• videotape presentations and view to self assess

Apprentice: *Set and Reach for Goals*

To introduce the concept of goal setting, discuss measurement tools with students Brainstorm and list the tools and devices, or better still, bring some into the classroom/library and give students an opportunity to manipulate them. e.g. rulers, tape measures, measuring cups, pedometer, light meter, thermometer, barometer, weigh scale, blood pressure monitor... Discuss with students the function and purpose of measurement tools. For example:

• The thermometer measures the temperature so we can decide how to dress to go to school,
• A blood glucose monitor indicates a person's blood sugar level. If it is too high or too low appropriate action can be taken.
• A speedometer measures how fast your vehicle is traveling so you know if you are holding up traffic or in danger of getting a speeding ticket.

Draw an analogy between these devices and the tools that students and teachers use to assess their learning progress. Help students to understand that assessment informs students and teachers what they are doing well and indicates areas that need attention. Using this information, students and teachers, with family support, can then make plans for improvement. They can carry out those plans, re-evaluate, and adjust their actions until learning goals have been met.

Goal Setting
• Identify areas for improvement.
• Set goals for self-improvement.
• Plan action for self-improvement.
• Re-evaluate and adjust strategies.

Gathering Evidence of Understanding

Try using some of the goal setting tools provided in this book, create your own, and invite students to create organizers to help with goal setting. Students should be able to analyze their own learning process, identify their strengths and weaknesses, and set goals for improvement. To maximize the impact of these goals make sure students revisit them, assess, and re-assess their personal progress. See Research Success Rubric Fig. 69-70, *Resource Check* Fig. 10, *Assessing My Effort* Fig. 71, *My Research Reflection* Fig. 72, *Planning for Improvement* Fig. 73.

Adaptations

Read stories about people who have set goals and through their efforts have made a real difference in the world e.g. Read a book about Terry Fox and his battle with cancer and the legacy he has left through the annual, International Terry Fox Run.

Start a bulletin board of other people who have set goals and accomplished their dreams.

Have students write stories, plays, poems, or use some other creative format to share their goals for the future.

InfoStar: *Apply New Learning and Take Action*

Every good inquiry should end with more questions. These questions could be sparked by interest in related but unexplored subjects the student is curious about. They could be questions about unsolved aspects of their inquiry. Students may want to know how they can share their learning with a wider audience.

They may see a link between what they have learned through their research and something they know from another context. Students could be so passionate about their inquiry that they now want to apply what they have learned and take action in their community. One excellent example is Craig Keilburger who, along with his older brother, is creating and promoting opportunities. See *Link Up*. Giving students the freedom and inspiration to take their inquiry another step provides opportunity for the ultimate level of learning, transfer. Transfer makes learning relevant.

Some Examples of Transfer and Apply
• Apply learning to another subject (use information from an environmental study to write a play to promote an environmental cause).
• Apply learning to a practical situation (read a manual and tune up a bicycle).
• Conduct further related inquiries (consider questions arising from the study of healthy lifestyles and conduct an investigation of recreational facilities in the community).
• Share learning with a wider audience (share learning electronically).
• Take informed action (request a meeting with a city planner to discuss an impact study).

Gathering Evidence of Understanding

Provide reflective prompts to nudge students to think about the importance of their work and what else they can do with their research results.

Transfer Prompts
• Why is my work important?
• Who is it important to?
• What difference does it make to me, to my community, to the world?
• Where do I go from here?
• How can I use this information?
• What else do I want to know?
• How can I find out more?
• Who can help me?

Research Success Rubric - Part One (Fig. 69)

Achievement Level	Develop Plan	Define Task	Locate Resources	Select Data
Level Four	- creates an effective plan independently - produces an accurate creative, visual representation of the plan - understands interdependence of stages of the research model and can explain it to others - uses appropriate software effectively to create an imaginative visual of plan	research question or statement - drives analysis and synthesis and pushes for application and/or transfer of new learning - leads to original insight	- resources extensive in number and variety, beyond those reachable through school sources, specifically focused to individual need - keywords and phrases very successful, expanding when necessary - variety of ICT's (phone, FAX, Internet OPAC) to locate resources - coached others who required assistance with ICT's	- specific data to support need, very comprehensive - all data relevant specific inquiry question/problem - evaluates all data and sources for authenticity, currency and bias
Level Three	- creates an effective research plan using prompts - produces an accurate visual of the plan - understands the interdependence of stages of the research model - uses appropriate technology to create visual	research question or statement - drives analysis and interpretation of information and could result in transfer - guides a search for personal meaning	- resources adequate in number and variety, relevant to specific topic - keywords effectively expanded when necessary - used a variety of ICT's, independently, to locate resources	- sufficient data to support need - data relevant to needs - evaluates all sources for authenticity, and currency
Level Two	- understands the research model and follows all steps of a prescribed plan - creates a visual with some assistance - demonstrates limited understanding of the stages of research model - uses software, with assistance, to create visual	research question or statement - requires collection of facts and other peoples' opinions (no interpretation) - asks for a " retelling"	- resources insufficient in number and variety, relate to general topic, not specific to need - keywords required expansion but not expanded - uses OPAC independently - requires assistance to use Internet	- more supporting data required - data related to general topic not specific - some data questionable (outdated, inaccurate, inconsistent - some attempt to evaluate sources
Level One	- omits steps of the prescribed plan - unable to create an accurate, complete visual of the research plan - no evidence of understanding of the research model - makes no use of technology	research question or statement - low level question/problem requiring just facts gathering, listing or mandate unclear - invites plagiarizing	- resources very limited in number, variety and relevance - keywords unsuccessful, no attempt for new search - requires assistance to use OPAC and Internet	- data insufficient - data too general or off topic - much of data invalid little evidence of attempts to evaluate data

Research Success Rubric – Part Two (Fig. 70)

Achievement Level	Process Information	Make Personal Meaning	Share New Learning	Assess Results Set New Goals
Level Four	- creates and utilizes sophisticated organizers to analyze and synthesize information - devises original strategies for working with information and testing ideas - creates sophisticated, task specific, organizers	- extrapolates connections and relationships to make new discoveries and hypothesis - makes personal connections to community and beyond and asks more questions	- shared very comprehensive, well organized, information - content effectively elaborated on the mandate - mode and style of presentation original and stimulated great interest	- creates effective criteria and or tools for self evaluation - defines a continuum to achieve future goals - has a plan for next steps and a vision for future goals
Level Three	- uses sophisticated organizers to analyze and synthesize information - sorts, classifies, compares, analyzes, tests ideas - creates simple organizers to work with information	- reflects on existing knowledge and new information to make connections and see relationships - makes personal links to new knowledge	- shares complete, well organized information with clarity - content specific to the mandate - demonstrates understanding of topic - presents information effectively and in an interesting manner	- applies provided criteria for honest and realistic self evaluation - identifies weakness or potential growth areas - plans logical, next steps achievable
Level Two	- uses simple teacher-made organizers - sorts and ranks data - creates simple organizers with assistance	- sees connections and makes relationships between old and new knowledge when guided - some attempt to make personal connections	- shares limited amount of information with minimal organization/clarity - content poorly focused - presentation failed to stimulate interest	- applies provided criteria unrealistically - goals show some relevance but require more specifics - plans and next steps unrealistic
Level One	- uses organizers with assistance - simply sorts data - makes no attempt to create organizers	- unable to see connections and make relationships between old and new knowledge - no evidence of personal connections	- shares incomplete, poorly organized information - content lacked clarity and focus - presentation is ineffective	- self evaluation incomplete - inappropriate or unrealistic goals - little evidence of plans for next steps

Assessing My Effort (Fig. 71)

Name:...

Date:..

Project:..

Project Tasks	What was I supposed to do?	How did I do?
Planning		
Organizing		
Managing my Time		
Working with others		
Gathering information		
Testing my ideas		
Sharing my project		
Setting new goals		
Overall		

My Research Reflections (Fig. 72)

I am proud of

Things that worked well

Things that didn't work out

I want you to know that

Things I did very well

Things I want to do better

Planning for Improvement (Fig. 73)

Project..................................Date............

Student Perspective

- Project focus
- Time management
- Organization
- Effort
- Results

Plans for improvement

1)

2)

3)

Family/Home Perspective

- Project focus
- Time management
- Organization
- Effort
- Results

Plans to help

1)

2)

3)

Teacher Perspective

- Project focus
- Time management
- Organization
- Effort
- Results

Plans to help

1)

2)

3)

Common findings and plans

Part 8: Adding it All Up

- ❑ How will we know we have succeeded at building our own Information Literate School?
- ❑ How will we track what we've done?
- ❑ What will we use to examine the scope and depth of our programs?
- ❑ What do we need to share with colleagues, administrators, and parents?

In this section you will find templates and organizers to help you gauge your success and make plans for the future.

Gauging Success at the Learner Level
- ❑ What evidence do you have that students are information literate?
- ❑ How can we measure the impact teaching information skills has on student achievement?
- ❑ What will we measure?
- ❑ Each InfoSkill task in this book is complete with a description of what students need to know and be able to do to demonstrate their ability and understanding of the skill. Find this information in the task section called *Gathering Evidence of Understanding*. For criteria to assess student achievement see *Documenting the Evidence* in the notes section of each task. Use these criteria to create rubrics, check lists, and other assessment tools.

Collect evidence of success at the learner level.
- ❑ student work- assess process, product, and effort
- ❑ completed organizers
- ❑ rubrics
- ❑ reflection/learning logs
- ❑ self/peer evaluation
- ❑ research folders
- ❑ source sheets
- ❑ checklists
- ❑ evidence of goal setting
- ❑ student conferencing notes
- ❑ video tape of students working or sharing
- ❑ photos of students working
- ❑ test results and reporting comments

Analyze this evidence over time to determine student growth and make adjustments to your program.

Gauging Success at the Teaching Unit Level

- ❑ How has unit design improved in the information literate school?
- ❑ Do some/all teachers integrate information literacy skills and information technologies in lesson design?
- ❑ What tools can teachers use to help them plan for improvement?

Sometimes the information activity will be a single lesson to support a curriculum topic. Other times it may be a complete research project. Whatever the situation, it will be carefully designed taking into account what the students need in order to achieve the targeted expectation or standard. Utilize the building tools in this book to help you plan and document your success. Collect and analyze data on your efforts and assess your progress. Make use of all opportunities to record and share your initiatives.

Collect evidence of success at the teaching unit level.

- ❑ collaboration logs
- ❑ records of debriefing of lessons/units
- ❑ copies of lessons and units
- ❑ documentation of skills taught over time
- ❑ workshops designed to help teach and integrate information literacy skills
- ❑ increased teacher confidence integrating technologies
- ❑ requests for resources, lessons, and other services ?
- ❑ repeat collaboration

Gauging Success at the Organization Level

Has the teaching and learning environment improved in the information literate school?
What changes have been made in the school library and the classrooms?

Collect evidence of success at the teaching environment level.

- ❑ circulation statistics
- ❑ collection mapping
- ❑ quality of collection (inclusive, curriculum support, print and electronic, variety, interests)
- ❑ budget reports
- ❑ student and teacher comments
- ❑ access to physical and virtual collection for all
- ❑ access to computers and other technologies
- ❑ before and after video or photos
- ❑ engaged, eager students and teachers

Bottom Line

Share your results! Continue to grow!

Analyze the evidence you have collected at all three levels. Decide what action needs to be taken and share your future plans with colleagues, administrators, parents, politicians, and other interest groups. Continue to reflect, rethink, and redesign; and your information literate school will continue the cycle of inquiry for improvement, just as information continues to expand in volume and complexity.

Ways of getting the message out:

- ❑ informal discussions with everyone who will lis
- ❑ formal meetings, forums and presentations
- ❑ professional portfolio
- ❑ action research projects
- ❑ newsletters
- ❑ information pamphlets
- ❑ reports/briefs
- ❑ workshops
- ❑ professional journal articles
- ❑ article or letter for a newspaper or magazine
- ❑ video footage
- ❑ contribute to/or create a web space

Based on Triangulation of Evidence-Based Practice.
Loertscher and Todd. *We Boost Achievement, 2003*

Building Tools

Research Project Design Fig. 74, This organizer will guide you as you design research and inquiry learning experiences for your students.

Build Your Own Research Template Fig. 75. Complete and file this planning organizer for each research unit you develop. Periodically review these documents to assess whom you have collaborated with and how often.

Build Your Own: InfoSkills Template Fig. 76. This helpful organizer prompts you to record a comprehensive overview of each information skill activity as well as provide documentation of the evidence of understanding and plans for improvement.

Build Your Own: Long Range Program Planner Fig. 77. Develop a bird's eye perspective of your program. Plan with the big picture in mind. To use this tool to its full potential take the time to record evidences of success e.g. conversations, stories, statistics etc.
Analyze the breadth and depth of your program on a regular basis, by month, term, and year.

Documenting the Evidence of Understanding Fig. 78. This chart will help you record and analyze the variety and effectiveness of the assessment tools you use. Plan to assess the process and the product as well as student effort.

Reflect, Rethink, Redesign Fig. 79. Keep track of your own thoughts as the lesson or unit progresses. Document your ideas about the experience at all three levels. Plan for improvement as you go along.

Library Media Specialist as Agent for Collaboration Fig. 80. This chart will to help you identify the effects of your collaborative efforts and make plans for improvement.

Collaboration Log Fig. 81.   Collect collaborative evidence to share with colleagues and administrators.

Let's Chat Fig. 82. This organizer provides a friendly framework for debriefing and assessing the success of a collaborative teaching and learning experience. Save these reflections, as well as ideas from informal conversations with teachers, to document the success of the experience at the teaching unit level.

InfoSkills Matrix Fig. 83 or 84. Use these in a variety of ways to:
- track teaching of information skills
- record grade and level of sophistication
- provide an overview of skills taught at a grade level
- provide an overview of skills taught across the grades
- provide an overview of skills taught in specific disciplines/subjects
- develop action plans
-

Research Project Design (Fig. 74)

Start with "The Backward Design Process" in *Understanding by Design* by Wiggins and McTighe

• Identify what it is you want students to know and be able to do.

• Determine what will constitute acceptable evidence of student learning

• Plan the learning experiences and instruction
  • Analyze the student expectations or standards identified to pinpoint the information processing skills students will need to be successful
  • Break down any mega skills into teachable micro skills
  • Decide on the level of sophistication for each skill
  • Apply the stages of your research model to organize and chunk the learning
  • Design lessons that will form scaffolding to enable students to build understanding and ultimately to construct knowledge.

• Reflect, rethink, redesign all through the process

• Gather evidence of success
  • Learner level
  • Learning unit level
  • Learning environment level

• Analyze and share the results

• Set goals and develop a plan for improvement

Teacher Designers need to consider that information tasks of all types require:

♦ A well defined purpose
♦ Clear assessment criteria
♦ A relevant real world challenge
♦ Engaging resources and strategies
♦ Learning experiences that build on one another to enhance understanding
♦ Feedback to students throughout the process
♦ Opportunities to work collaboratively
♦ A repertoire of information literacy skills
♦ Access to a variety of resources
♦ Access to information technologies
♦ Scaffolding (e.g., visual organizers, prompts)
♦ Strategies to model reflective learning (e.g., journals, learning logs)
♦ Opportunities to demonstrate understanding
♦ Opportunities to self assess and set goals for improvement
♦ Collaboration with a teacher librarian/media specialist

Build Your Own - Research Project Template (Fig. 75)

Curriculum Context	Criteria for Assessment

Targeted Information Skills	Assessment Tools
Define and Clarify	
Locate and Retrieve	
Select Process and Record	
Analyze	
Synthesize	
Share and Use	
Reflect Transfer and Apply	
Collaboration Notes	

Build Your Own: InfoSkills Template (Fig. 76)

Info Skill

☐ Novice
☐ Apprentice
☐ InfoStar

Curriculum Context

Resources & Equipment

Learning Experiences

Gathering Evidence of Understanding

Next Time

Documenting Evidence of Understanding
☐ Learner Level
☐ Teaching Unit Level
☐ Organization Level

Build Your Own – Long Range Term Planner (Fig. 77)

Teaching Information Literacy	Evidence of Success

Building Reading Literacy	

Enhancing Learning Through Technology	

Collaboration with Teachers	

Post Analysis	

Documenting Evidence of Understanding (Fig. 78)

Plan to assess throughout the research process. Use a variety of assessment tools and assessors. Make a logical match between the tool and task The underlying purpose for assessment is to gather data about student performance. This information will be used to inform students and teachers so action can be taken to improve both the teaching and learning process.

Use this checklist to plan and track types of assessment.

Purpose – D (diagnostic), F (formative), S (summative)

Assessor – T (teacher), P (peer), S (student)

Class/es

Date													Effectiveness
Rubric													
Checklist													
Rating Scale													
Conference													
Anecdotal Record													
Response Journal													
Learning Log													
Questionnaire													
Multiple choice test													
True/False Quiz													
Matching Quiz													
Cloze activity													

Analysis

Reflect, Rethink, Redesign (Fig. 79)

Unit/Lesson:	Reflect	Rethink	Redesign
Learner Level			
Learning Unit Level			
Learning Environment Level			
New ideas			

Don't forget

Library Media Specialist - an Agent for Collaboration
(Fig. 80)

Collaborative Activity	Evidence of Collaboration	Benefits for Students
- discover topics being studied in classrooms & provide resources - reaches out to teachers to offer support - points out interconnections of information skills and content standards	- surveys staff about topics and units being taught - listens to staffroom, playground, parking lot, comments and diplomatically and enthusiastically offers to teach information skills and gather resources -	- accesses information sources at a variety of reading levels - more engaged, interested and motivated than usual - more successful
- provide motivational reading opportunities	- surveys student interest and skill levels - stocks appropriate and reading - gives exciting book talks - posters, displays, reviews, award winners - hosts book clubs	- piqued interest levels - lots of material to choose from - something for everyone
- integrate information skill instruction as needed for curriculum content	- plans and teaches strategic skill lessons for classes - provides resources to support curriculum - sources related fiction, articles, artifacts, career information...	- learns skills in context - learns skills necessary for achievement in content areas - makes real world connections
- provide access to digital information beyond the library	- consults with teacher regarding time slots - schedules to accommodate classes as needed - bookmarks appropriate sites - teaches supporting information skills - provides in-service training in related information skills for teachers	- accesses material not available in hard copy - accesses material beyond the school collection - learns to evaluate websites and materials - more options, more levels, more perspectives
- partners with teachers to plan and teach unit s of instructions	- makes long range plans to accommodate teachers and classes e. g. *Build Your Own Long Range Planner* - utilizes planning and tracking templates e.g. *Build Your Own - Research Template, InfoSkills Matrix* - maintains a *Collaboration Log, Let's Chat* chart, - team teaches	- lower pupil teacher ratio - more positive experiences with materials at skill level - more learning styles accommodated - practices, learns, more skills in less time - observe collaboration and its benefits in action
- assesses learning experience considering planning, teaching and learning	- maintains a *Let's Chat* chart, *Documenting Evidence of Understanding* chart - compare partner units to	- marked on process as well as product - benefits from two or more perspectives on effort and achievement - continually improving learning experiences
- provide in-service training to teachers	- offers informal sessions for teachers at lunch and after school - introduces new materials, programs, hardware to staff	- receives greater support from teachers - accesses newer better resources - assisted by more teachers who understand their needs

Collaboration Log (Fig. 81)

Week/Month.....................................

Type of Collaboration and Teacher(s) Names	Unit Title / Curriculum Focus	Grade Level	Library Time	# of Students
Totals/Summaries				
Patterns Observed				
Proposed Actions				

Based on *Reinventing Indiana's School Library Media Program in the Age of Technology*, Loertscher 2001

Let's Chat
Collaborative Teaching and Learning Experience (Fig. 82)

Library Media Specialist(s)……………………………………
Teacher(s)………………………………………………………..
Unit Title……………………………………Grade……………………….# of
students……………………………

Focus Area	Reflections	Next Time
Teaching Curriculum Expectations		
Teaching Information Literacy Skills		
Building Reading Literacy		
Enhanced Learning through Technology		
Library Collection/Facility		
Student Engagement		
Collaboration		

InfoSkills Matrix (Fig. 83)

Class Experiences: Subject/Grade/Teacher

Skill\Level	N,A,I	N,A,I	N,A,I	N,A,I	N,A,I	N,A,I	Tallies and notes
Define and Clarify							
Understand the research process							
Explore topic							
Define a research topic							
Develop questions							
Develop keywords							
Develop a plan							
Locate & Retrieve							
Use search strategies links							
Locate relevant resources							
Skim, scan, consider							
Evaluate							
Design surveys							
Collect information from primary sources							
Select Process & Record							
Pre reading activities							
Read, view, listen							
Select relevant data							
Compare sources - fact from fiction							
Read pictures							
Read non-fiction text							
Note-making							
Legal & ethical use of information							
Analyze							
Graphic organizers							
Sort							
Compare							
Classify							
Investigate, identify patterns, trends							
Respond to text							

Make connections						
Determine cause effect						
Determine, identify, predict, impact						
Interpret, infer, predict						
Identify, examine perspectives						
Work collaboratively						
Synthesize						
Consider alternatives, test ideas						
Point of view, form and opinion develop and argument (propaganda)						
Develop generalizations						
Draw conclusions						
Share and Use						
Decide on best format						
Develop product/presentation						
Utilize appropriate technologies						
Test Ideas						
Communicate Ideas						
Reflect, Transfer & Apply						
Reflect on process/product						
Self evaluate						
Set goals						
Recognize importance of learning- personal, community, global connections						
Apply learning						
Take informed action						
Tallies and analysis notes						

InfoSkills Matrix (Fig. 84)

Class Experiences: Subject/Grade/Teacher

Skill\Level	N,A,I	N,A,I	N,A,I	N,A,I	N,A,I	N,A,I	Tallies and notes
Define and Clarify							
Locate & Retrieve							
Select Process Record							
Analyze							
Synthesize							
Share and Use							
Reflect, Transfer & Apply							
Tallies and analysis							

Index

In this index, the reader will find the titles of each InfoSkill, the titles of each figure, and the subject of each InfoSkill.

InfoSkill Task Subjects and Levels Index

This table provides an additional access point to all the infoskills by level and by curricular area.

Page	InfoSkill	Novice p,j,i,s	Apprentice p,j,i,s	InfoStar p,j,i,s
1	**Define and Clarify**			
2,3	Understand the Research Process	language arts j	science j - i	careers i - s
4,5	Explore a Topic	science p	social studies i	world studies i- s
8,9	Define a Research Topic	geog i	science j	guidance i
12,13	Develop Questions	language arts - grammar p-i	language arts , literature p-j	career studies i-s
14,15	Key words	history j-i	science j	dramatic arts s
16,17	Develop a Plan	science p-j	social science i	media arts i-s
	Locate & Retrieve			
24,25	Search Strategies	science j-i	geography i-s	information technology j-i- s
28,29	Locate resources	language arts p	science jr	geography jr int sr
32,33	Skim, scan, consider	language arts j	social science j	careers i-s
34,35	Evaluate Resources	language arts p- j	civics i-s	physical education, health i-s
40,41	Design surveys	mathematics, health i	science j	media studies i-s
46,47	Use Primary Sources	social science j	social science p	history i-s
	Select Process & Record			
48,49	Pre-reading Strategies	environmental studies i-s	geography i	science j
56,57	Actively Read, View, Listen	social studies j	science j-i	social science s
62,63	Select Relevant Data	science p-j	geography i-s	global issues i-s
66,67	Determine Fact	science p	science i	global issues i-s
70,71	Read Pictures	social studies j	language arts p	visual arts i-s
72,73	Use Features of Non-Fiction Text	science i	social studies j	technology j
76,77	Note-making	science j	history i	literature i-s
82,83	Legal and Ethical Use of Information	arts j-i-s	english i-s	literature i-s
	Analyze			
90,91	Use Organizers	language arts p	science j-i	social studies j-s

94,95	Sort	social studies p-j	science j	technology i-s
98,99	Compare	social studies j	science j-s	geography i-s
102,103	Classify	science j	geography i	history i-s
108,109	Identify and Investigate Patterns Trends	literature p,j,i,s	health j	global issues i-s
112,113	Respond to Text	science j	language p-j	economica i-s
116,117	Make Connections	art j-i	history i	dramatic arts i-s
120,121	Cause & Effect...	science p	science j	history i-s
124,125	Impact	science i	science j	history i-s
130,131	Interpret, Infer, Predict	social studies j-i	history i-s	current events i- s
136,137	Understanding Perspective	language j	science & technology i-s	media studies i-s
140,141	Collaborate	geography i-s	social studies j	language j
	Synthesize	Strategy	Strategy	Strategy
146,147	Synthesize	model conferencing to synthesize	use organizers to synthesize	design organizers and thinking process maps
	Share and use	Strategy	Strategy	Strategy
156,157	Share and Use	teacher selected and modeled products/presentations	guided planning and writing of information text	student choice and plan
	Reflect Transfer and Apply	Strategy	Strategy	Strategy
166,167	Reflect Transfer and Apply	reflect and self evaluate	set and reach for goals	apply new learning and take action
	Adding it All Up	Learner Level	Teaching Unit Level	Organization Level
173,174	Adding it All Up	gauging success and collecting evidence of success	gauging success and collecting evidence of success	gauging success and collecting evidence of success

Key
p K-3
j 4-6
i 7-9
s 10-12+